Native American Biographies

SACAGAWEA
WESTWARD WITH LEWIS AND CLARK

Alana J. White

Enslow Publishers, Inc.

44 Fadem Road	PO Box 38
Box 699	Aldershot
Springfield, NJ 07081	Hants GU12 6BP
USA	UK

For Erin.

Library of Congress Cataloging-in-Publication Data

White, Alana, J.
    Sacagawea: westward with Lewis and Clark / Alana J.White.
      p. cm. — (Native American biographies)
    Includes bibliographical references and index.
    Summary: Profiles the life and times of Sacagawea, with an emphasis
on her journey taken with the Lewis and Clark Expedition.
    ISBN 0-89490-867-7
    1. Sacagawea, 1786-1884—Juvenile literature. 2.Shoshoni women—
Biography—Juvenile literature. 3. Shoshoni Indians—Biography—Juvenile
literature. 4. Lewis and Clark Expedition (1804-1806)—Juvenile literature.
[1. Sacagawea, 1786-1884. 2. Shoshoni Indians—Biography. 3. Indians of
North America—Biography. 4. Women—Biography. 5. Lewis and Clark
Expedition (1804-1806)] I. Title. II. Series.
F592.7.S123W48   1997
978'.004974'0092—dc20
  [B]   96-22359
                                            CIP
                                            AC

Printed in the United States of America

10 9 8 7 6 5 4 3 2

Illustration Credits: American Philosophical Society, p. 108; Denver
Public Library, Western History Department, pp. 20, 23, 33, 37, 71, 95,
112; Kae Cheatham/SunSpot, p. 45; Map by Jerry Tracy, pp. 11, 49, 67;
Montana Historical Society, Helena, p. 59; Oregon Historical Society,
#55621, p. 78; Oregon State Archives, Highway Division Records, Photo
3295, p. 85; University of Oklahoma Press, p. 6.

Cover Illustration: The State Historical Society of North Dakota.

Contents

AUTHOR'S NOTE

In 1805–1806, a young Shoshone woman accompanied Meriwether Lewis and William Clark on an expedition to the Pacific Coast. The young woman's name was Sacagawea. In those days, white Americans considered the lands west of the Missouri River a "wilderness." For a group of explorers to make their way to the ocean and safely back was a great triumph. As news of the Lewis and Clark Expedition spread, so did Sacagawea's fame. Many writers inaccurately called her Lewis and Clark's pathfinder. Some even said she acted as ambassador to Native Americans the travelers met on their long trek across the North-American continent. These are exaggerations. Most modern historians agree, however, that Sacagawea made many important contributions to the expedition—contributions that helped ensure its overall success. Imagine a sixteen-year-old with a baby in a cradleboard on her back, beginning a journey that would take her some six thousand miles by foot, horseback, and canoe on the first organized exploration of the American West. This is her true story.

— ❖ —

In this sketch, Native American artist George Henry drew Sacagawea as he thought she might have appeared as a young mother. Her dress, the baby's cradleboard, and the leather bit worn by the pinto pony are Shoshone in design.

THE ADVENTURE BEGINS

The cold river water gleamed in the spring sunshine as the men on shore made last-minute preparations for the long journey west. Into the boats went guns and ammunition, food, and medical supplies. Sacagawea, too, had prepared for the trip. That April of 1805, Sacagawea was about sixteen and married to a French-Canadian fur trapper almost three times her age. She was a brand new mother. During the months ahead, the baby boy would need clean bedding and clothes. These had been packed in the child's cradleboard, a wooden frame worn on the back, used by many Native American women for carrying infants. Inside, the baby's belongings would be safe and dry.

✦Lewis and Clark Lead the Way✦

Sacagawea's husband was Toussaint Charbonneau. Meriwether Lewis and William Clark, the two leaders of the exploring party that had arrived on the river the previous fall, had hired Charbonneau to go cross-country with them to the western sea (the Pacific Ocean). Charbonneau could communicate with many of the Native American tribes the exploring party was sure to meet as it traveled.

Lewis and Clark considered Charbonneau a man of no particular merit.[1] Today, some historians think the two men hired him just because they wanted Sacagawea to accompany them on the expedition west. From the Hidatsa and Mandan tribes, Lewis and Clark had heard about the Rocky Mountain range they would have to cross to reach the Pacific Ocean. To cross those mountains, they would need horses. Sacagawea was Shoshone, a member of the tribe that lived for a short time each year on the near side of the Rockies. Clark had noted this fact in his journal.[2] He and Captain Lewis hoped Sacagawea could help them bargain for Shoshone horses when—and if—they met the Shoshones in the Rocky Mountains.

❖Sacagawea's True People❖

Shoshones were Sacagawea's true people. When she was about twelve, she had been captured by the raiding Hidatsa warriors (also referred to as "the Minnetarees"). They frequently swept across the plains to steal horses from the Shoshones when they came down from the mountains to hunt buffalo. The Hidatsas named their captive Sacagawea, or Bird Woman. They took her far from her home in the Rocky Mountains to the place where they and the Mandans lived in villages high atop the bluffs that overlooked the Upper Missouri River (near present-day Bismarck, North Dakota). There Charbonneau either bought Sacagawea or won her from the Hidatsa chief, perhaps in a gambling game.[3]

In October 1804, as the winds began blowing in from the North, the Lewis and Clark Expedition, also called the Corps of Discovery, had appeared like a strange vision on the cold waters of the Missouri River near the Mandan and Hidatsa villages.[4] The explorers had quickly selected a site and begun building a fort where they would spend the winter. Meriwether Lewis was a melancholy and moody young man, while the red-haired William Clark was good-natured and outgoing.[5] Their sudden presence in the vicinity of the villages had aroused the curiosity of their Native American neighbors. "Soon after our arrival many men womin & Children flocked down to See us," Clark reported in his notes.[6] (William Clark, like

Meriwether Lewis, followed his own individual style of spelling and punctuation.)

❖The Louisiana Purchase❖

Using interpreters, Lewis and Clark held councils with the chiefs and village elders, explaining the purpose of the expedition. Just one year before (1803), the American government had purchased a vast amount of land west of the seventeen—at that time—American states. Acquired from France, the land was known as the Louisiana Territory. For $15 million, the United States had doubled its size. President Thomas Jefferson wanted Lewis and Clark to explore the territory and to determine if there was a usable water route across the North-American continent. President Jefferson, Lewis and Clark explained, was the Great White Father who would protect the Mandans and Hidatsas if they would trade with the Americans rather than with the Spanish and the French.[7]

Exploring the West had been in the back of Jefferson's mind for a long time. He had moved ahead with plans for an expedition and put Lewis—who had been his private secretary—in command. For his partner in the expedition, Lewis had chosen William Clark. Both Lewis and Clark were from Virginia—Thomas Jefferson, who lived at Monticello, was Lewis's close neighbor. Meriwether Lewis was born on August 18, 1774. In school his studies included mathematics and geography. When he was

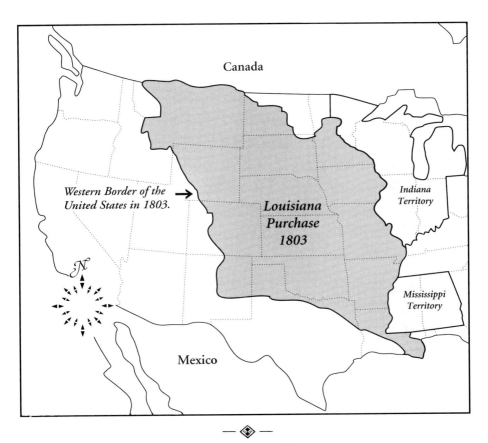

In 1803, the United States purchased the Louisiana Territory from France, opening the way for Meriwether Lewis and William Clark's expedition west.

thirteen he took over the management of the family plantation. Within five years, he was a gentleman farmer and the head of the household. During the Whisky Rebellion of 1794, he volunteered for duty in the Virginia militia. Later he signed on with the regular army.[8]

◈Who Were Lewis and Clark?◈

William Clark's background was significantly different from that of Meriwether Lewis. Clark was born on August 1, 1770. As a boy, Clark moved with his family from Virginia to Louisville, Kentucky. Clark probably had little formal schooling. Surrounded by wilderness, he became an expert hunter and woodsman. In the 1780s Kentucky was still part of the frontier. These were trying times for the settlers and for the Native Americans who deeply resented this invasion of their land. At the age of nineteen, William Clark joined one of the local militias formed to protect American citizens. He became an expert riverboat man and rifle shot. He learned how to draw maps, build forts, and command men. Eventually, like Meriwether Lewis, he joined the regular army.[9]

Lewis and Clark met at the small frontier outpost of Fort Greenville, where Clark was Lewis's commander. Within a few months, Clark left the army and returned to Kentucky. The pair kept in touch. When Lewis invited Clark to share his command of the western expedition, Clark accepted with enthusiasm.

"My friend," he wrote in answer to Lewis's letter, "I join you with hand and heart."[10]

One setback came when Congress failed to make William Clark a captain like Meriwether Lewis. Instead, they assigned Clark the lower grade of second lieutenant. This infuriated Lewis, but he could not change the situation.[11] He assured his friend that they would share the leadership of the expedition, no matter what Congress said. The other men of the Corps would never know the truth. That is exactly what they did.

❖The Journey Begins❖

The Corps of Discovery began the first leg of its journey on May 14, 1804. The men of the Corps started up the Missouri River from a camp near the village of St. Louis. Most of our knowledge of the Lewis and Clark expedition—and of Sacagawea—comes from several journals that Lewis and Clark kept as they traveled. In them, the two captains recorded daily events and drew maps for Thomas Jefferson. At President Jefferson's request, they made notes on the plants and animals they observed. They also wrote extensively about the culture of the Native Americans they met on their way to the Pacific.

Throughout the bitterly cold winter of 1804–1805, the Mandans and Hidatsas welcomed members of the Corps into the warmth of their lodges. Wearing snowshoes, the explorers went with their new friends to hunt buffalo. They shared meals and participated in many unique tribal rituals.

On Christmas day the Corps celebrated with a festive holiday party. The men raised the American flag and fired guns. They ate, danced, and drank brandy. Sacagawea was present as they frolicked and she watched them with amusement.[12]

❖ Sacagawea's Son Is Born ❖

By now, she and Charbonneau had moved into Fort Mandan. On February 11, 1805, their son was born in a log cabin there. In his journal, Captain Lewis described Sacagawea's labor as tedious and the pain violent.[13] René Jusseaume, a French-Canadian trader who had been hired as an interpreter during the stay at the fort, helped Sacagawea. To hasten the birth of the child, Jusseaume recommended giving Sacagawea a potion made from two rings of a rattlesnake, finely ground and mixed with water. Captain Lewis supplied the rattlesnake rings. Within a few moments, the baby was born. Named Jean Baptiste, the child sometimes was called Pomp.

The weather continued to be cold and harsh. There was not always enough to eat, and severe cases of frostbite occurred in the villages. The Missouri River was frozen solid. Throughout February, the explorers struggled to free their boats from the thick ice. After several days of chopping with axheads tied to long poles, the men finally worked the canoes loose and got them on land for repairs.[14]

At last, spring arrived. The Corps began making final preparations to begin the second leg of its journey. On April 7, 1805, Lewis and Clark gave the go-ahead: today was the day of departure. The expedition was about to enter a vast, uncharted land. The men readied the vessels and exchanged farewells with the Mandans and the Hidatsas who had come to see them off.

What of Sacagawea? Captain Lewis, especially, seems to have taken the advice the Hidatsas had given him and Clark to heart: If they expected to cross the Rocky Mountain barrier and reach the Pacific Ocean, the white men would need those Shoshone horses. Sacagawea, Lewis believed, was their only chance of getting them.[15] The Hidatsas were correct.

Although some early historians felt free to speculate that Sacagawea was excited by the trip, there is no proof of that. The most that may be said is that, after five years of captivity, she was at last heading back toward the Rocky Mountains and the land of her Shoshone people.

CAPTURED!

Sacagawea had been picking berries near a cool stream with the other Shoshone women and children when the Hidatsa war party, armed with guns and on horseback, swooped down on them. Shoshones had horses, but they were not warlike, and they did not have firepower. They scattered. Many women, men, and boys were killed. Some Shoshone men, realizing they were outnumbered, mounted their horses and fled. Sacagawea ran for the river. She was halfway across, making her way through a shallow place, when Hidatsa pursuers overtook her.[1]

❖Sacagawea Taken by Hidatsas❖

The Hidatsas claimed many prisoners that day. One of Sacagawea's good friends, Jumping Fish, was among them. The two girls comforted each other and shared the hardships of captivity. Then Sacagawea's friend escaped. The youngsters had little hope of ever meeting again. Some of the popular accounts of this incident claim that Sacagawea could have escaped, too. Instead, the story goes, she remained behind to take care of another girl who was sick. No one knows if this is true. Like so much else about Sacagawea's life, her childhood is cloaked in mystery.

❖Sacagawea's Early Life❖

Sacagawea was most likely born around 1789 to Northern Shoshone parents who lived on the western slopes of the Rocky Mountains in present-day Idaho. When she was about twelve, her people traveled east across the Rocky Mountains to hunt buffalo and antelope. Today, the place where they camped is known as the Three Forks of the Missouri (in present-day southwest Montana).

The Hidatsas raided the Shoshone camp to steal horses as well as take prisoners. Horses had arrived in the southwestern region of the North American continent about one hundred fifty years earlier. This was when the Spanish conquest moved north from Mexico. The Native Americans living in the Southwest traded goods for the Spanish horses. They also captured strays. As these people began trading horses with their northern neighbors, horse ownership spread. This sparked an immense change in the Native American way of life. With horses, tribes could attack—or escape—their enemies with great speed. In addition to catching rabbits with nets and tracking antelope, they could follow the great buffalo herds farther and faster than they could on foot.[2]

❖The Shoshone People❖

When the Spaniards first appeared in North America, the Shoshones were nomads. They roamed the desert in an area called the Great Basin, west of the Rocky mountains. Traveling in small bands, the Basin Shoshones looked for food and lived in temporary shelters. Although horse ownership dramatically changed the lifestyle of most Native Americans, it did not change the people living within the Great Basin. Few buffalo were to be found in this unfriendly desert area. Also, the horses ate some grasses necessary to the diet of these people. Other Shoshones did embrace the opportunity to own horses. There were, for example, Eastern Shoshones, who moved south and became Comanches.[3]

Shoshones who moved on toward the mountains became known as Northern Shoshones. These were Sacagawea's people. The horses the Hidatsas stole from them on the day of Sacagawea's capture most likely were pintos and Appaloosas. Shoshones may

— ◈ —

This painting by Karl Bodmer depicts the action and danger of the buffalo hunt. In warm weather, armed with bows and arrows, Native Americans rode onto the plains. The buffalo provided not only food, but also hide and fur for clothing.

have acquired the Appaloosas from their neighbors to the west, Nez Perces, who were known for training and breeding them.[4]

Like Shoshones of the Great Basin, Sacagawea's people moved with the seasons in search of food. They did not plant crops, however. Unlike their desert kin, the Northern Shoshones usually did not live in lodges made of grass, but in tipis, or skin-lodges.[5]

Along with fish, Sacagawea's nation depended on roots and seeds for food. Using crooked sticks with curved ends, they dug up prairie turnips (a kind of artichoke) and ate them boiled. They gathered berries, bluish-black and fruitlike, and made them into cakes. From ground sunflower seeds, they made flour. From the flour, they made bread. The boys hunted with their dogs and brought home cottontails, groundhogs, squirrels, ducks, and other small game. Nothing was wasted. Uneaten food was dried and preserved for winter. With fur pelts and animal skins, the women made blankets, robes, leggings, and moccasins.

Like people everywhere, Sacagawea's people enjoyed relaxation and games. The most popular games were dice-throwing and a hand game played with bones or sticks. Foot races, horse races, and wrestling were also popular. When it came to marriage, young men and women were permitted to find a mate for themselves. Sometimes, though, families arranged a match . Once a couple began living in the same shelter, they were considered married.[6]

◈Surviving the Winter◈

In wintertime, life for Sacagawea would have been especially hard. Often the hunters who went out on snowshoes to track elk, deer, bear, and mountain sheep returned empty-handed. During these cold, snowy months, people sometimes starved. In every season, death and sickness were frequent. The buffalo Sacagawea's people hunted provided not only food, but also hide and fur for warm clothing. Although the hunt was dangerous, it was important—important enough to coax the Northern Shoshones down the eastern slopes of the Rocky Mountains and into the open, where they knew other tribes might attack them for their horses. They might also be taken as prisoners of war. This is exactly what happened to Sacagawea.

◈A New Life Begins◈

Following their raid on the Shoshone camp, the Hidatsas took Sacagawea and their other captives hundreds of miles east to their home on the Upper Missouri. With these people, Sacagawea had a brand new life. The Hidatsas lived in villages near their neighbors, the Mandans. Unlike the Shoshones, the Mandans and Hidatsas were not wanderers. They had permanent homes. These were round, earth lodges with log frames covered with sod and thatch. The lodges were large enough to house several families

— ❖ —

The winters where Sacagawea lived in present-day North Dakota were harsh with cold. Karl Bodmer's Dog Sled on Frozen River *shows a Native American woman using a dog sled to carry goods, as well as a child, across the frozen Missouri.*

and their horses, protecting them from bad weather and enemy attack.

At first, Sacagawea may have been permitted some freedom enjoyed by other young girls, but soon she was put to work to help older Hidatsa women. For their fires, the Hidatsas needed wood. To find it, the women crossed the Missouri River in bullboats, round vessels made from basket work covered with buffalo hides. These compact runabouts would have been new to Sacagawea. For crossing narrow bodies of water, her people used rafts made from small reed bundles.

There was another basic difference between Sacagawea's tribe and the Hidatsa and Mandan people. The Hidatsas and Mandans were farmers as well as hunters and trappers. With the changing seasons, they planted corn, squash, pumpkins, and beans. Young girls planted and tended. Girls helped harvest crops. Unlike the Shoshones, when the Hidatsa men returned to their villages from the buffalo hunt, farm tools had to be made.[7]

◈Sacagawea Marries◈

No one knows exactly how long Sacagawea lived as a captive before becoming one of the wives of Toussaint Charbonneau. Many historians believe she was with the Hidatsas for about five years before the fur trapper either bought or won her and then married her. Sacagawea's husband was born in or near Montreal, Canada, around 1759. As a young man, he made his living among fur traders on the frontiers. Later, he was employed by the North West Company, a London-based fur-trading organization that flourished in Canada and the Great Lakes region.[8] Eventually, Charbonneau traveled to Mandan and Hidatsa country, where he worked as an interpreter. These two tribes had been welcoming white traders to their villages for many years. Both French and British traders often came down from Canada to barter guns and other goods for furs.

Like Meriwether Lewis and William Clark, the Mandans and Hidatsas did not have much respect for Charbonneau. They mocked his bragging and rough ways by giving him insulting nicknames like Chief of the Little Village and Forest Bear.[9] Apparently, Native Americans who knew Charbonneau did not think him capable of governing a large village. Also, they considered him as untamed and rough as a bear. Still, Charbonneau had been living peacefully among the Hidatsas for several years when the Lewis and Clark Expedition appeared on the Upper Missouri River in the fall of 1804.

❖The Expedition Continues❖

The Corps of Discovery, traveling in canoes and a fifty-five-foot long keelboat, had created a flurry of excitement in the villages upon its arrival there. There was the keelboat itself—Native Americans had never seen anything quite like it. Its swivel gun fascinated them. So did Captain Lewis's air gun and the small iron hand mill for grinding corn the white explorers had brought with them. Of special interest was William Clark's African-American slave, York.

❖William Clark and York❖

The first Native Americans that the expedition had encountered as it traveled up the Missouri River from St. Louis had not been too impressed with the dark color of York's skin. Some of these natives had seen black men before. Further upriver, however, York had caused a stir. The Arikaras had regarded him with open-mouthed astonishment. They, as well as the Mandans and Hidatsas, considered York great medicine, a term these tribes reserved for unexplainable mysteries. York seems to have taken the attention good-naturedly. He let the Native Americans he encountered rub his skin with their fingers to see if he was a white man painted black. He played with the Native American children, pretending to chase after them as they followed him around. All through the winter of 1804–1805, York remained on good terms with Mandans and Hidatsas. On New Year's Day he, and others of the Corps, entertained Mandan villagers by dancing. Of York's relationship with Sacagawea, little has been written. One thing is certain, however. The two shared a common bond. They were the only members of the exploring party—official or otherwise—who were considered the property of another person.[10]

◈Charbonneau Joins the Expedition◈

Toussaint Charbonneau did not waste any time before offering his services to the leaders of the Corps of Discovery for a fee. Meriwether Lewis and William Clark arrived in the vicinity of the Mandan and Hidatsa villages in late October 1804. Just one week later, Clark noted in his journal that Charbonneau wished to hire on with the expedition as an interpreter. Clark added that Charbonneau had said his two "Squars" were Snake Indians.[11] One of the two Snake Indians Clark referred to in his journal was Sacagawea. In describing Sacagawea to Clark this way, Charbonneau had used one of several descriptive names given to the Shoshone nation by white people as well as by some Native Americans. The original use of the word "snake" probably was due to a misunderstanding of the word "Shoshone" in sign language, a swift, snakelike motion of the hand. In those days, too, it was common for white people to refer to Native American women as squaws.

In addition to Meriwether Lewis and William Clark, other men of the Corps kept journals. On November 4, 1804, Sergeant John Ordway wrote that two Shoshone women had brought the captains a gift of four buffalo robes. Quite likely, Sacagawea was one of the two women who, along with Charbonneau, visited the camp that chilly Sunday.[12]

Clark's journal entry indicated that Toussaint Charbonneau had more than one wife. Charbonneau, who was part Iroquois, was following a practice accepted at that time among some Native Americans. When Lewis and Clark met him, in addition to Sacagawea, Charbonneau was married to at least one other young Shoshone woman. She was probably called Otter Woman.

Another of the few written mentions of Sacagawea comes from Meriwether Lewis's journal entry of February 7, 1805. By then Charbonneau, his fellow interpreter, René Jusseaume, and their wives had moved into Fort Mandan. When a guard told Captain Lewis the women were allowing visitors inside the walls of the fort late at night, the captain ordered locks put on the gate. Relations between the members of the Corps and the natives nearby were friendly enough, but Captain Lewis remained ever-protective of his men.

❖The Journey Heads West❖

Soon after this incident, the expedition made preparations to leave Fort Mandan and embark on the journey west. At the last moment, Sacagawea almost did not go. About the middle of March, 1805, her husband announced to Lewis and Clark that he would not accompany the expedition unless the captains met a list of his demands. Charbonneau would work only as an interpreter, he said. He would not do labor under any circumstances. He would not stand guard. He could quit the expedition whenever he wished, taking with him all the provisions he needed. Lewis and Clark refused Charbonneau's demands: they would do without his services. A few days later, the interpreter apologized. He would perform the same duties as the other men.

In his journal entry of April 7, 1805, Lewis wrote that the expedition was about to enter a country at least two thousand miles wide on which the foot of white men had never trod. As he listed the interpreters setting out with the party that windy spring day, he referred to Sacagawea, calling her the wife of Charbonneau. She was, the captain noted, traveling with a young child.[13] As Lewis wrote those words, Sacagawea's baby, Jean Baptiste, was not quite eight weeks old.

Into the Unknown

The Corps of Discovery left Fort Mandan in six canoes and two flat-bottomed dugouts, called pirogues. In the white pirogue rode Sacagawea, most likely clothed in a fringed deerskin dress.[1] Baptiste was in the cradleboard on her back. Besides passengers, the white pirogue carried Lewis and Clark's scientific instruments and papers. These items were vitally important to the explorers. President Thomas Jefferson had directed the captains to study and record everything they saw on their journey to the Pacific. At the same time that the Corps headed west, the keelboat that had accompanied them as far as the Mandan and Hidatsa villages was heading back south to St. Louis. The keelboat was loaded with papers and reports, ceremonial buffalo robes, a live prairie dog, and several magpies, all for the enlightenment of the president.

❖To the Pacific Ocean?❖

In addition to conducting scientific studies, Lewis and Clark were seeking the answer to a burning question: Was it possible to reach the Pacific Ocean by following the rivers of North America? If so, riches from the Orient could be shipped across the Pacific, then transported by boat east over the continent to the United States. This would strengthen the economy of the young nation.

President Jefferson had other things on his mind as well. The Scottish-born Canadian explorer Alexander Mackenzie had reached the Pacific by traveling Canadian rivers in 1793. Mackenzie's passage through the mountains had been extremely difficult. His route was impossible for trade. Still, Jefferson found Mackenzie's achievement disquieting. He did not want the United States falling behind in exploration.[2]

At long last, the expedition was leaving Fort Mandan. What lay ahead in the West? For the most part, the land they were entering was uncharted. There were few maps available. Tales were told of

— ◈ —

Karl Bodmer's painting shows Mandan women crossing the Missouri River. In the background are earth-covered lodges of the Mandan settlement.

volcanoes and a mountain made of salt. There were those who believed a lost tribe of Welsh people lived in the far western reaches of the region. Some spoke of a race of giants.[3]

◈Along the Missouri River◈

In the early nineteenth century, most Americans knew very little, if anything, about the vast mountain range that formed a barrier to the Pacific. Drawing pictures in the dirt with sticks, the wide-ranging and knowledgeable Hidatsas assured Lewis and Clark that, yes, the mountains were there. What Lewis and Clark did not know was the massive size of the shining Rocky Mountains. Nor did they realize the full danger of crossing the steep, narrow mountain ridges and finding a pass before the snow came.

Following the Missouri River, the Corps set forth, pushing across modern-day North Dakota on foot and by canoe. The party numbered thirty-three. Along with Lewis and Clark, there were Sacagawea, Charbonneau, and the baby, Baptiste. The other civilians included York and a hunter who was an expert in sign language. In addition, twenty-six young soldiers had been handpicked for the voyage. Also along was Lewis's frisky Newfoundland dog, Seaman.[4] (Although for many years writers have referred to Lewis's pet as Scannon, today historians know his true name.)

❖Finding Roots to Eat❖

Ever the impatient rambler, Lewis usually walked alone or went off hunting with a few men.[5] Clark spent the greater part of each day walking alongshore with Sacagawea, Charbonneau, and the baby.[6] Sacagawea made her first recorded contribution to the party two days into the trip, when she dug up some edible roots hidden by small animals in piles of driftwood. The roots, which resembled artichokes, provided a welcome treat for the men, whose principal diet was meat.[7]

Less than one week later, on April 13, 1805, Sacagawea and her family were in the white pirogue, with Toussaint Charbonneau steering. Suddenly, a gust of wind blew up on the river. Alarmed, Charbonneau rocked the boat, endangering everyone aboard. Lewis ordered the two sails taken in. Within moments, the pirogue was secure. The accident, Lewis wrote in his journal, could have cost them dearly. When it occurred, the white pirogue—which they considered their safest and steadiest vessel—was two hundred yards from shore. The waves of the Missouri were high. If the boat had overturned, all aboard probably would have died.[8]

❖Entering Montana❖

Finally, the travelers reached the junction of the Missouri and Yellowstone rivers. The Yellowstone was within thirty miles of where the Hidatsas had placed it when they drew their maps in the dirt. The Corps took this as a good sign—they were headed in the right direction. Each man had a bit of whisky. Pierre Cruzatte, one of the French members of the Corps, played his fiddle, and the men danced in celebration. Leaving the Yellowstone behind, the explorers proceeded up the Missouri. On April 27, 1805, they left present-day North Dakota and entered the future state of Montana.

✦Near-Disaster Strikes✦

The Corps was near present-day Crooked Creek when another sudden burst of wind struck the white pirogue. Sacagawea was in the rear of the boat with Baptiste. Once again, Charbonneau was at the helm. In a panic, he dropped the tiller and cried to God for mercy. This time, Lewis and Clark were on shore. They fired their guns and shouted orders across the water. Pierre Cruzatte—the fiddler—threatened to shoot Charbonneau if he did not immediately take hold of the rudder. Two men bailed water.

Sacagawea, probably waist-high in cold Missouri water, scooped up the goods rapidly washing overboard. At last, the men managed to haul in the sail and row safely to shore. Acting calmly and quickly, Sacagawea had saved books and clothing, a magnet, a microscope, and the captains' journals. Lewis wrote warmly of her when he recorded this story. To him, Sacagawea was loyal and brave.[9] As for her husband, Lewis called Charbonneau the worst steersman of the party and maybe the most timid waterman in the world.[10] And no wonder! A few days later, the two captains named a branch of the Musselshell River Bird Woman's River, probably in honor of Sacagawea.[11]

— ◈ —

This detail by Edgar S. Paxon shows Sacagawea in a type of fringed deerskin dress. Lewis and Clark probably named a branch of the Musselshell River, Bird Woman's River, in honor of her.

The party traveled on, beset by a series of hair-raising experiences. A rattlesnake almost bit Clark. A campfire started a blaze that brought a tree crashing down among the tents. Seaman chased after a beaver in the river, was bitten in the leg, and almost bled to death. One night a buffalo stumbled across the white pirogue and rushed into the sleeping camp, its sharp hooves just missing the heads of the men. The buffalo charged the tipi the Charbonneaus shared with the captains. Seaman jumped out, barking. Into the darkness the buffalo thundered, leaving the camp in an uproar.

◈The River Splits◈

Nearly exhausted, in early June 1805, the party reached a point in the Missouri where the river split into two branches. This was an unexpected turn of events. The Hidatsas had told Lewis and Clark they would come to a great waterfall beyond which the Rockies lay. But which fork led to the waterfall? They had to locate the correct branch and cross the mountains before the autumn snows.

Small parties scouted the two forks of the river. Finally, the captains decided Lewis would follow the south branch with a few men and try to find the waterfall. While he was gone, Sacagawea fell dangerously ill.

❖Sacagawea Becomes Sick❖

To protect her from the hot rays of the sun, William Clark moved her to the covered part of the white pirogue. He gave her medicine and applied bark poultices. Sacagawea became steadily weaker. Upon his return to camp, Captain Lewis gave Sacagawea water from a nearby spring and kept her on medicine. In his journals, he wrote of his personal concern for Sacagawea, who had Baptiste in her arms. He also noted that she remained the expedition's only chance of obtaining Shoshone horses.[12]

Within a couple of days, Sacagawea was well enough to gather some apples. She ate the apples raw, along with some dried fish. The wind blew violently that day. Her pain and fever returned. Captain Lewis, who had put her on a strict diet, scolded Charbonneau sharply.[13]

The next day, Sacagawea was stronger. She even went fishing. On June 24, 1805, Lewis reported her perfectly recovered.[14] There was more good news. While exploring the south branch of the river, Lewis had found the great falls the Corps had heard about. The Corps of Discovery could proceed along this branch confident that it would lead them to the Rocky Mountains. Lewis had found not one waterfall, however, but five. The distance around the falls, Clark determined, was eighteen miles.

◈Navigating the Falls◈

They could not possibly make it over the falls in their boats. Instead, they planned to carry their boats and supplies around the falls on land. Such a maneuver is called a portage. Portaging the Great Falls of the Missouri, as we call the place today, meant building wagons to carry the canoes and supplies around the cascading water. The soldiers of the Corps had been chosen because they were young and strong. By now, however, the rigors of the expedition had taken their toll. The party had suffered colds and other sicknesses. Clothes were ragged, moccasins thin. Thousands of buffalo had moved across the muddy landscape around the waterfalls, leaving the ground sharp and pointed. Cactus pricked the feet of the men as they towed the canoes every step of the way. Wagon wheels gave. Ropes, now much used and ragged, broke. Still, the men did not complain.

◈A Storm Brings Trouble◈

One morning during the long portage, Sacagawea and her family accompanied Clark on foot in the direction of the first waterfall. The small group was walking along the river when Clark noticed a black cloud rising in the west. He hurried everyone into the safety of a ravine. A torrent of rain and hail more violent than anything he had ever seen began to fall. A wall of water rushed toward them.

Sacagawea had Baptiste in her arms. Charbonneau had already scrambled to safety. He attempted to pull Sacagawea up out of the ravine by the hand, but was so scared he could scarcely move. Clark quickly put his gun and shot pouch in his left hand and with his right pushed Sacagawea and the baby before him. A torrent of water swept through the ravine, shoving mud and boulders before it.

York was searching for the others. Their condition alarmed him greatly. To revive them, he gave them spirits from his canteen. The raging water had washed away Baptiste's cradleboard, along with all his bedding and clothes. Clark directed the party to run quickly for camp. Clothes could be found there to cover the young mother and child. Sacagawea was, he wrote, just recovering from a severe illness. She was wet and cold, and he feared a relapse.[15]

The camp was in confusion. The hail had hit the men with terrible force, battering and nearly killing some of them. The plains were so wet that evening that nothing more could be done as far as transporting boats and goods around the giant waterfalls. Preparing for and conducting the eighteen-mile journey around the Great Falls of the Missouri cost the explorers one month of precious time. On July 15, 1805, behind schedule, bruised and tattered and sharply aware that with each passing moment the mountains were growing colder, the explorers proceeded on.

Reunited

The Corps of Discovery left the Great Falls of the Missouri and traveled upstream along the eastern edge of the Rockies. Almost at once, Meriwether Lewis and William Clark began to see what they called Indian signs. Captain Lewis spotted a village of deserted willow shelters. He assumed that the inhabitants had been Shoshone. This fueled his hope of soon meeting Sacagawea's people. William Clark noted a number of leather lodges. Judging from their appearance, the lodges had been inhabited the previous fall.

✦Where Were Sacagawea's People?✦

While watching for Shoshones, Lewis and Clark continued to make lengthy notes in their journals about plants and animals they discovered. The sunflower was in bloom and abundant, elk and buffalo plentiful. Captain Lewis was fond of the berries growing in the region, particularly the yellow (golden) currant. He preferred them to the currants growing in his own garden.[1]

Some members of the expedition walked and hunted game. Some paddled, poled, and towed the canoes upriver. The land was beautiful, but crossing the mountainous country posed a serious challenge. Hoardes of mosquitoes and gnats attacked the Corps, forcing its members to sleep beneath gauze tents. The ground was covered with flint that cut and bruised the feet. Prickly pear was in bloom, Lewis wrote. " . . . Their thorns are so keen and stif that they pearce a double thickness of dressed deers skin with ease."[2] One evening, sitting by the light of the campfire, Clark pulled seventeen cactus needles from his feet.

Earlier that day, the boats had passed through a canyon where the river appeared to have forced its way through solid rock. Captain Lewis called the gorge the gates of the rocky mountains (near present-day Helena, Montana).[3] Emerging into a valley on Saturday, the Corps sighted smoke rising from the plains. Was this a signal from one Native American

— ◈ —

On July 18, 1805, Sacagawea and the Corps passed through a canyon in present-day Montana where the river seemed to have forced its way through solid rock. In his journal, Captain Meriwether Lewis called the gorge the Gates of the Rocky Mountains.

party to another concerning the strangers sailing upriver? Might the Corps be near the Shoshones? It certainly seemed so.

William Clark already had seen the remains of several willow brush camps. These were more recent than the brush camps he had spotted the previous week. Bark had been peeled from the nearby pine trees. Sacagawea told the captains that her people did this to obtain the sap and soft part of the wood and bark for food.[4] They were probably starving, Lewis thought. Why else would they eat the wood of a tree?[5]

✦Sacagawea Recognizes the Area✦

On Monday, July 22, 1805, Sacagawea recognized the countryside. This was where the Shoshones visited the banks of one of the nearby creeks to get white earth for paint, she said. Her relations lived on this river. Furthermore, the place where three rivers came together to form the Missouri was near. This cheered the men, for it verified their belief that they were on the correct route.[6]

✦Three Forks of the River✦

The Corps of Discovery was now within the mountains. Here shallow water and rocky rapids made the going rough. The two captains often struck out in different directions, seeking Shoshones. Sacagawea, they discovered, was right: three days after she told them they were near the river junction, Clark, along with a few other men, reached the Three Forks of the Missouri. Lewis and the main party caught up with him two days later. The captains named the three streams the Jefferson, the Madison, and the Gallatin, after President Thomas Jefferson, James Madison, secretary of state, and Albert Gallatin, secretary of the treasury.

Clark, who scouted the north fork another twenty-five miles, was fatigued, his feet blistered and wounded by prickly pear thorns. Charbonneau had gone scouting with Clark and added to the lieutenant's difficulties. The interpreter gave out, his ankles failed him. He was unable to continue. The next day, Clark was extremely ill from heat and dehydration. Still, when the river threatened to sweep Charbonneau away, Clark rescued the man, saving his life. William Clark was not the only member of the expedition with problems. Needle and thread grass carpeted the thin soil of the high lands. Its barbed seed penetrated moccasins and leather leggings. The barbs made Seaman miserable.[7]

❖In Search of Horses❖

Lewis was becoming increasingly anxious about the future of the expedition: ". . . if we do not find them [the Shoshones] or some other nation who have horses," he wrote on July 27, "I fear the successfull issue of our voyage will be very doubtfull. . . ."[8]

The goal of the Corps remained fixed: they had to discover a passage over the Rockies leading to a branch of the Columbia River. The plan was to navigate the branch of the river they found to the Columbia. Then they would follow the Columbia to the Pacific. They did not know the scope of the mountains. From the looks of the surrounding countryside, even if the branch of the river they found proved navigable, timber might not be available for canoes. Still, Lewis and Clark hoped for the best.

◆ Nearing Sacagawea's People ◆

Sacagawea gave the captains startling news the following day when she told them they were camped on the spot where five years earlier the Hidatsas had kidnapped her. Walking upriver a short distance with Captain Lewis and Charbonneau, Sacagawea indicated the place she was overtaken in midstream. Lewis wrote in his journal:

> She does not . . . show any distress at these recollections, or any joy at the prospect of being restored to her country. For she seems to possess the folly or the philosophy of not suffering her feelings to extend beyond the anxiety of having plenty to eat and a few trinkets to wear.[9]

As Lewis and Clark soon were to discover, the sixteen-year-old was actually more emotional about the situation than they might suspect.

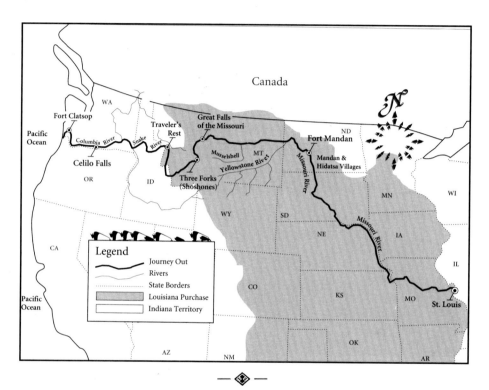

The Lewis and Clark Expedition began its journey in St. Louis.
From that riverfront town, the Corps of Discovery sailed the
Missouri to the villages of the Mandans and the Hidatsas.
With Sacagawea along as interpreter, the Corps headed
west, making its way to the Pacific Ocean. This map shows
the present-day states the party passed through as it traveled.

For several days, Lewis and Clark investigated the Three Forks. Finally, they decided that the Jefferson, coming as it did from the southwest, was the next river to follow. The Corps proceeded on. When the Jefferson split into three branches, the captains chose the main river, now called the Beaverhead. On August 8, 1805, Sacagawea recognized a high hill off to the right. This point, she said, was not far from the summer retreat of her nation, on a river beyond the mountains that flowed west. On this river, or on the river immediately west of its source, they would find her people.[10]

Without horses, the Corps would have to store a great many of its supplies, supplies already small in number given the probable length of the voyage yet to come. Encouraged by Sacagawea's words, Lewis struck out on foot. The captain was determined to find Native American horses if it took a month! Clark was still suffering from a boil on his ankle. He could not walk far. He stayed behind, in charge of the main party. Sacagawea, like Clark, remained with the canoes.

Slowly, Clark and his companions progressed up the Beaverhead. The river was shallow and swift. The legs of the men wading the water, pushing and hauling the canoes, ached with cold. Tempers flared. One evening during dinner, Charbonneau struck Sacagawea. For this, Clark reprimanded him severely.[11]

Walking on shore the next day, Sacagawea and Clark barely escaped being bitten by rattlesnakes. Clark named the place Rattlesnake Mountain. The men were complaining of fatigue. Enduring the freezing river water and living on deer meat, which was poor and had a distinctive bitter taste, were taking their toll. Lewis had been gone a week. "I have no Accounts of Capt Lewis Sence he Set out . . ." Clark wrote on August 15, 1805.[12]

The following day, Sacagawea provided the men with a welcome treat. While walking along the shore she, Clark, and Charbonneau found some berries. Sacagawea gathered the ripe fruit in a pail. At noon, when Clark's party stopped in a grove of cottonwood trees, she shared the berries with the others.[13]

❖Sacagawea Finds Her People❖

Then, something extraordinary happened. On the cold morning of August 17, 1805, Sacagawea, Charbonneau, and Clark left camp and were walking alongshore when a group of mounted Shoshones rode toward them. Sacagawea danced with delight and made signs to Clark—these were her people! A small Shoshone camp was nearby. As Sacagawea approached it, a young woman darted from the crowd with her arms outstretched. She and Sacagawea embraced—this was Jumping Fish, who had been taken prisoner with Sacagawea but who afterwards was able to escape from the Hidatsas. The meeting touched Clark deeply. Sacagawea and Jumping Fish expressed such joy, he wrote. This was a truly interesting situation.[14]

When Lewis returned, he told Clark about finding the main Shoshone camp. The Shoshones had been suspicious of Lewis when, using sign language, he had indicated that a larger party led by another white chief (Clark) was coming upriver. Lewis wanted the Shoshones to go with him to meet the party so that they could begin trade. Suspecting an ambush, the Shoshones had accompanied Lewis with reluctance. In fact, they had refused to go with him at all until he told them a Shoshone woman was with the water party and would make the explorers intentions clear. While Sacagawea visited with her childhood friends, Lewis and Clark held council with the Shoshone chief, Cameahwait. Cameahwait seated Clark on a white robe and tied white shells resembling pearls in Clark's red hair. As a sign of peace, the men removed their moccasins and smoked the pipe passed around the tent.

Lewis and Clark held a council. Sacagawea was called on to interpret. She was beginning to speak when suddenly she jumped up, ran to Cameahwait, and embraced him, weeping. Here was another almost unbelievable coincidence: Chief Cameahwait was her brother. The two spoke briefly. Sacagawea returned to her seat and tried to interpret for the men, but her tears interrupted her frequently. After the council, Sacagawea learned that everyone in her family but Cameahwait, another brother who was not present, and her small nephew was dead. Following Shoshone custom, Sacagawea adopted the boy. No further mention of this child is made in the journals. Some historians assume that when the expedition once again got underway, Sacagawea left him with his two uncles.[15]

There was also a Shoshone warrior who stepped forward and declared that Sacagawea had been betrothed to him when she was a child. Told that the young woman was married and had a baby, the man dropped the matter.[16]

❖Trading for Horses❖

During a second council, Lewis explained the purpose of the expedition. The United States government was friendly, he said, and stressed the advantage of trade between the two nations. The expedition needed to find the best route to the land beyond the mountains. Lewis requested horses and a guide. Gifts were distributed—Jefferson medals, tobacco, mirrors, and beads. Everything about the Corps astonished the Shoshones, from their weapons and canoes to the African American, York, and the intelligence of Lewis's dog Seaman.[17]

As suspected, Sacagawea's people were starving. Constantly harassed, they moved about the rugged mountains and were living on the berries and roots they gathered in the plains. Yet, Clark wrote, they were not beggarly, but generous.[18]

Chief Cameahwait promised to trade for horses. The Shoshones gave the Corps alarming descriptions of the Lemhi and the Salmon Rivers that the captains had hoped to navigate to the Columbia. Waterfalls were abundant, the Shoshones said. One waterfall was higher even than the falls of the Missouri. No deer, elk, or any other game roamed there. Also, as the captains had suspected, there was no timber large enough for the construction of canoes.

Determined to discover for himself if the next leg of the river route was so forbidding, Clark set out with a party of eleven men to investigate. Five days later, he had his answer: they had no choice but to cross the Rocky Mountains on foot—and on horseback. Horses were absolutely vital. Time was ticking away. Fall was approaching, and they had already seen snow on the mountains.

Lewis and Clark eventually traded with Sacagawea's people for twenty-nine horses. They filled their canoes with stones and sunk them in the Lemhi River. They planned to retrieve the canoes on their return from the Pacific. On August 30, 1805, after loading the horses with the baggage, they started north on a road running along the river.

◈Sacagawea Leaves Her People◈

Sacagawea rode from the Shoshone camp on horseback. With her was six-month-old Baptiste. Now that Sacagawea had found her people, why did she leave them? Some historians have claimed that her decision to remain with the Corps of Discovery shows her loyalty to the expedition. There is no written record, however, stating that Sacagawea had a choice in the matter. Only one thing is certain. Toussaint Charbonneau was her husband, and Charbonneau was going to the Pacific.

Using axes, the Corps chopped a path through thickets and pushed up the rocky hillsides. Horses slipped, fell down the steep slopes, and were crippled. Rain pelted the expedition, followed by snow and sleet. In his journal, William Clark described September 4, 1805, as a very cold day. Snow blanketed the ground. Everything was wet and frosted. The Corps, he added, was prevented from breaking camp and getting underway that morning until the covering for the baggage thawed.[19] It was not a promising beginning.

Across the Rugged Rockies

The Corps trudged on. Shivering with cold, late on the afternoon of September 4, 1805, the party descended into a wide valley near present-day Sula, Montana. Here they saw a number of lodges belonging to the Salish nation. Today, the Salish speakers are usually called Flatheads, as Meriwether Lewis and William Clark called them. In fact, it never was customary for the people of this tribe to flatten their heads.

❖Welcomed by the Flatheads❖

Like the Shoshones, the Flatheads were friendly. They draped white robes over the shoulders of the explorers and with them shared the peace pipe. The Flatheads were so welcoming that the party camped near the tribe for several days. Soon the Flatheads would be leaving this place to meet Sacagawea's people at the Three Forks of the Missouri River. Like the Shoshones, the Flatheads were traveling to buffalo country east of the Rockies.

Using interpreters, Lewis and Clark held a council and passed out medals. They attempted to explain the purpose of the expedition. Communication was almost impossible, however. To the white men, the speech of the Flatheads sounded like the noise of a parrot. The Flatheads were light-skinned. Could the Flatheads be the lost Welsh tribe rumored to live in the wilderness? At least one man of the Corps was convinced of this.[1] Captain Lewis made a vocabulary list of the tribe's language. He also collected information about the people for President Thomas Jefferson.

According to Flathead legend, the white explorers were an astonishing sight to the tribe, as was the black man, York. They believed York had painted himself with charcoal, following the custom of Flathead warriors who were victorious in battle. This black man, they concluded, was the bravest man in the expedition.[2]

❖Getting More Horses❖

Three Eagles was the Flathead chief. Three Eagles presented Lewis and Clark with otter furs and antelope

— ✦ —

In this painting by Charles M. Russell, the Corps of Discovery meets friendly Native Americans in present-day Montana. Sacagawea is seated in the grass on the far right with her baby son, Baptiste, in the cradleboard on her back.

skins. His people had nothing much besides roots and berries to eat, but shared their food, nonetheless. They owned about five hundred elegant horses. The explorers purchased some of these and exchanged their sick animals for healthy ones. They now owned forty horses and three colts.[3]

On a rainy Friday afternoon, the expedition packed up its gear and once again got underway. The Flatheads left camp, too, on the way to the three forks of the river and buffalo country. In accordance with Flathead custom, before separating from the Corps the tribe shared information with Lewis and Clark about the best route across the Rockies to the western side of the mountains.[4]

Sacagawea and the explorers traveled north along the river the captains named the Bitterroot for a plant they found in the area. Before tackling the mountains, they camped for two nights at a spot they named Travelers Rest Creek (now Lolo Creek). They were out of flour. They were low on corn and berries. A Shoshone guide, whom they called Old Toby, and his son were with them. Old Toby warned Lewis and Clark that farther up in the mountains game would be hard to find, so while some of the men repaired clothing, others went hunting. Quite likely, Sacagawea had sewing and laundry to do for herself as well as for Charbonneau and little Baptiste.[5]

◆Over the Rocky Mountains◆

On September 11, 1805, the Corps started up Travelers Rest Creek over the Bitterroot Mountains of the Rockies, following the trail used by Native Americans to cross the mountains on the way east. Today, this is called the Lolo Trail. High, rugged hills and snow-covered mountains surrounded them. The trail along the mountain ridges was steep and stony. The exhausted horses lost their footing on slippery rims and rolled over with their loads. As Old Toby had warned, game was scarce. One afternoon the hunters killed only one prairie hen, which Lewis called a pheasant.

❖A Streak of Bad Luck❖

On Friday, September 13, 1805, the Corps began a run of bad luck. Captain Lewis lost his horse. Old Toby led the party astray for several hard miles before finding the trail again. The men were half-starved. On Saturday, for want of meat, they cooked one of the colts and ate it. Clark's horse was carrying Clark's desk. On Sunday, the horse stumbled, rolled down the mountain for forty yards, and lodged against a tree. The desk broke. The horse escaped without harm, however.[6]

Snow dropped from the pine trees. Snow hid the trail and soaked the members of the Corps to the skin. The weather was so cold Clark feared his feet would freeze in his moccasins. How did Sacagawea, traveling with a baby, manage these terrible conditions? No one knows.

With one companion, William Clark forged out ahead of the others and built campfires in preparation for their later arrival. At dusk the rest of the Corps showed up at Clark's camp wet, cold, and hungry. For supper, they killed a second colt. Desperate for food, Clark set out with an advance hunting party in hopes of finding provisions. That night, he and his men camped by a stream. Because they had nothing to eat, Clark named the stream Hungry Creek. On the second day out, the hunting party happened upon a stray horse. They butchered, cooked, and ate part of it. The remainder they tied from a tree for Captain

Lewis and his party. The Corps came upon the horse beef (as Lewis called it) the following day. The meal comforted the stomachs of the men. Sacagawea refused the meat. Her people found the idea of eating dogs and horses repellent.[7]

◈ Clark Crosses the Mountains ◈

Two days after striking out on their own, William Clark and his six hunters descended from the mountains and emerged onto a wide plain dotted with the lodges of the Nez Perces. For the advance party, the grueling trek across the Bitterroot range of the Rocky Mountains was over. Clark and his men were near Weippe Prairie, in present-day Idaho. Sacagawea, along with Lewis and the rest of the Corps, was still in the mountains.

On the plain, Clark came upon three young boys who ran from him and hid in the tall grass. Swinging from his saddle, Clark handed his gun and reins to his men and gave the three boys some ribbons. These gifts the boys took to their camp. A short while later, a Nez Perce man cautiously greeted Clark and his men. He then led them to a lodge in the village. Here, the villagers served a meal of buffalo meat, dried salmon, berries, and camas roots. At this time of year, the Nez Perce women were digging camas roots and drying them for winter food. The plentiful roots were heaped in huge piles on skins about the plains. In later years, William Clark drew a map naming this place Quamash, or Camas, Flats. The men ate heartily. That night, Clark was sick. After being so hungry, he had eaten too freely of the new food.

❖Waiting for Lewis to Arrive❖

While awaiting Lewis's arrival, Clark presented his Nez Perce hosts with a few gifts. Early the next morning he sent his men out to hunt deer. He gathered information about the surrounding countryside, the people, and the big river (the Columbia), which flowed into the Pacific. The hunters returned empty-handed. Clark purchased what little food he could from the natives and sent it back to Lewis and the rest of the party. On September 22, 1805, Captain Lewis and the others arrived at the Nez Perce village having happily triumphed, Lewis wrote in his journal, over the Rocky Mountains.[8] On the edge of starvation, Lewis and the other men rejoiced at the sight of the food offered them. Eating their fill despite Clark's warnings, they promptly got sick.

Using sign language to explain where they came from and that they desired peace, the captains held a council. They passed out Jefferson medals, flags, knives, handkerchiefs, and other gifts. In trade, they added to their store of supplies dried roots, bread, berries, and fish—as much as their weak horses could carry. The men of the Corps traded old tin canisters for dressed elk skin. From the skins, they made new shirts to replace their tattered clothing. One rainy, windy evening a Nez Perce chief, Twisted Hair, invited Lewis and Clark into the shelter of his lodge and gave them broiled salmon to eat. That night a great number of Native Americans were all around the explorers, Clark wrote.[9]

❖Mapping the River Route❖

For two weeks, Sacagawea and the Corps of Discovery camped near the Nez Perces along the Clearwater River. This was the third group of Native Americans, previously unknown to white people, the explorers had come into contact with in just over a month.[10] Chief Twisted Hair cheerfully gave them valuable travel information. On a white elk skin, the chief drew accurate maps of the three rivers the Corps would navigate on the way to the ocean. From the Clearwater, they would take the Snake River. The Snake would lead them to the Columbia. This journey, the chief indicated, would require about twelve days.

Lewis and Clark believed that the Nez Perces were friendly from the start. The truth was that at first the Nez Perce did not know what to make of these white men with hair on their faces. According to Nez Perce oral tradition, they thought seriously about ambushing and killing the explorers as they wound their way across the snowy mountains. Why they did not is told in at least two Nez Perce stories. In one of them, an elderly woman of the tribe who had been treated kindly by a white trader spoke up for the Corps.[11] Another story tells of a woman who, like Sacagawea, was captured by an enemy band, but managed to escape. This woman was befriended by the white people she met as she made her way hundreds of miles back to her people. For this reason, the story goes, the Nez Perces welcomed Lewis and Clark to their lodges.[12]

❖Making Canoes❖

When the men who had been ill were physically able, they chopped down some ponderosa pines and made four large canoes and one smaller one for the upcoming voyage down the Clearwater. This they did the Native American way, by burning out the tree trunks rather than hollowing them with axes and chisels. In secret caches, they hid their saddles and ammunition. They rounded up the remaining horses and branded them with a hot iron bearing the legend "U.S. Capt. M. Lewis."[13] The Nez Perces promised to tend the horses until the explorers returned on their way back to the United States. By October 7, 1805, the expedition was ready to take on the Clearwater, the first of the three rivers they hoped would transport them to the Pacific Ocean.

The Corps left camp accompanied by three Nez Perce men. One acted as guide. Lewis and Clark expected a fairly easy trip down the Clearwater River. Within a few hours, however, the Corps had passed ten rapids. One canoe hit a rock and sprang a leak. Later, another canoe sank. This meant stopping to repair the damaged boat and drying out water-logged supplies. The Shoshone guides, Old Toby and his son, had accompanied Lewis and Clark this far. Apparently, however, they were not fond of this means of travel. Within a few days, they left the expedition without stopping to collect their pay.

❖Reaching the Snake River❖

Sacagawea and the Corps of Discovery battled the Clearwater for four days. Finally, the expedition reached the Snake River. Here, as along the Clearwater, the Native Americans the explorers encountered were curious and friendly. They came from all directions to see the travelers. They even gave them a noisy farewell party the night before the Corps turned its canoes down the Snake.[14]

For six days, the Corps rode currents that one of the men wrote were "swifter than any horse could run."[15] On the Snake, the expedition faced a succession of tumbling, swirling rapids. Canoes dashed off hidden rocks. One chilly afternoon a canoe passing through a rapid smashed into a rock, filled with water, and sank. The crew clung to the rock. In about an hour, the men were rescued to a nearby island. Bedding, tomahawks, shot pouches, and clothing were lost. The soggy wet baggage was placed in the sun to dry.

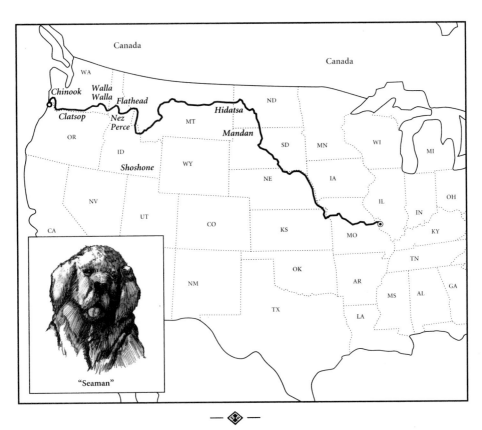

"Seaman"

Shown here are the names of some of the Native American tribes the Corps met as it traveled west across the North American continent. In present-day Idaho, Sacagawea was reunited with her people, the Shoshones. Also pictured is Meriwether Lewis's pet dog, Seaman, who accompanied the Corps to the Pacific Ocean and back home again.

On the island, the explorers happened upon a cache of split timber securely covered with stone. They had made it a rule not to take anything belonging to the Native Americans, without trading for it. Now, however, they took wood to build a fire.

While navigating the Snake River, the Corps passed many groups of Native Americans camped on the river banks, fishing the waters for salmon and drying their catch on huge scaffolds. The explorers exchanged beads and other trinkets for salmon. The fish provided a much-needed supplement to their skimpy diet of roots and berries. Salmon was not enough, however. To add meat to their diet, they traded for dogs. To Lewis, dog meat tasted better than any venison or elk. It was healthier, too. Unlike Lewis, Clark had no appetite for dog.[16] Using canines for food repulsed many western Native Americans, including Nez Perce, as well. With contempt, they called the explorers "dog eaters."[17]

Although we know Sacagawea would not eat horse or dog meat, we do not know how she felt about traveling the treacherous Clearwater and Snake rivers with her baby. For some time she is not mentioned in the journals at all. On October 13, 1805, William Clark did note in his writings that Sacagawea's presence with the Corps calmed Native Americans as to the friendly intentions of the expedition. A woman with a party of men, he explained, was a sign of peace.[18]

BIG WATER, BIG FISH

At last, the Columbia River! The Corps of Discovery had conquered the Clearwater and the Snake Rivers. What the group did not know when it reached the Columbia was that this mighty river would challenge it with even more dangerous rapids and waterfalls. While the Corps was at the Snake and Columbia River junction, several hundred Native American men came to visit, singing and beating drums. The group formed a half circle around the strangers, who made the usual signs of peace and distributed gifts.

❖A Welcoming Committee❖

The Native Americans welcoming Lewis and Clark were Palouse, related to the Nez Perce by language. Twisted Hair and Tetoharsky, two Nez Perce chiefs who had joined the explorers on the Snake River, had pressed on ahead with news of the expedition. For a couple of days, Lewis and Clark remained at the junction, gathering information and recording it for President Thomas Jefferson. Then the explorers left the Snake and canoed down the Columbia. Once again, they saw many Native Americans fishing for salmon and drying their catch on wooden racks along the river bank. From these people, the Corps purchased fish and berries. (From one tribe they also traded for forty dogs that rode downriver with them, along with Seaman. These extra dogs were for food.)

Many Native Americans gathered on the river banks to watch the Corps pass by in canoes. Others, however, frightened by the appearance of white people, ran and hid. Coming upon a village of deserted lodges along the river one day, Clark decided to investigate. He opened the door of one lodge and found its inhabitants, many of them women and children, crying and wringing their hands in terror. Clark greeted them in a friendly manner and gave them the few gifts in his pockets. Tensions did not ease, though, until the Corps came into sight on the river with Sacagawea in one of the boats. Women did not accompany war parties. As in the past, Sacagawea's presence confirmed the explorers friendly intentions.

— ❖ —

This painting by Karl Bodmer shows a Native American village with tipis and the Rocky Mountains in the distance. While traveling to the Pacific Ocean, Sacagawea and the Corps of Discovery camped near similar villages.

The two Nez Perce chiefs traveling with the Corps explained the people's fears. On his way to the lodge, Clark had shot a crane and then a duck with his rifle. These people had never heard a rifle blast. The sound had terrified them and convinced them the white intruder was a creature fallen from the clouds.[1]

❖More Challenges Ahead❖

A few days after this incident, Sacagawea and the expedition faced another test: the roaring Celilo Falls. The Corps unloaded the canoes and carried the empty boats and the baggage around the foaming barrier. With ropes of elk skin they lowered the boats over huge rocks and paddled on, ready for the next challenge. The sight of the swirling water of the Short Narrows of the Columbia shocked William Clark. Here the great Columbia, bound by rocks on either side, narrowed to a channel about forty-five yards wide. To the amazement of the Native Americans gathered on the rocks above the river, the Corps shot the canoes safely through the wild rapids.[2]

At the Long Narrows, the river channel cut through rough black rock. The swollen water churned. The Corps was in a hurry to reach the Pacific Ocean, but after considering the risk posed by the Long Narrows, took the time to portage valuable baggage and supplies. Below the Long Narrows (today the Short and Long Narrows are know as the Dalles of the Columbia), the expedition made camp.

Twisted Hair and Tetoharsky had stayed with them past the two narrows. Now it was time to say good-bye. The captains paused in their work to bid the two Nez Perce chiefs farewell and smoke with them in friendship.

◈ Life on Land ◈

During this brief respite from the river, members of the expedition hunted, repaired the leaky canoes with resin collected in the woods, and dried wet supplies in the sun. One evening, after an exchange of gifts with visiting Native Americans, Lewis and Clark had a fire built in camp. Pierre Cruzatte played the fiddle and York danced. The visitors enjoyed the entertainment so much, they spent the night. All was not merry, however. On the morning after the party, Clark argued with Sacagawea's husband about the man's duty to the expedition.[3]

Once again, the voyagers were on their way. At villages along the Columbia, they spotted brass kettles, a cutlass, which was a short sword used by sailors, a British musket, and Native Americans wearing sailors jackets. These goods must have come from the British and Yankee ships that traded with the Native Americans along the coast. Surely the Pacific was near. Between the Corps and the sea, however, loomed the Cascades of the Columbia. Pelted by rain, for two days the explorers battled jagged rocks and pounding rapids. At last the river widened and slowed. The party camped within sight of Mount Hood, Mount St. Helens, and Mount Washington. They had made it through the last mountain range standing between the Columbia and the Pacific Ocean and entered the dense rain forest of the Northwest Coast.[4]

The waterfalls and rapids were behind Sacagawea, but the weather on the coast was wretched. Days were dark and cloudy. Thick fog hid the view across the river. On November 7, 1805, the fog finally cleared. "Ocion [sic] in view!" Clark wrote. "O! the joy."[5] The body of water Clark saw that day was not the Pacific but the mouth of the Columbia River. As he recorded his observation, the Corps was just east of present-day Astoria, Oregon. The Pacific remained a good twenty miles away. Still, the members of the expedition could hear the ocean waves pounding the distant, rocky shore.

❖The Columbia River❖

Cautiously, the Corps probed the northern shore of the Columbia. At this time of year, along with hail and thunder came fierce winds. Huge pieces of driftwood crashed toward the canoes. High swells on the river and the rolling motion of the dugouts made Sacagawea seasick. Decent campsites were almost impossible to find, firewood scarce. Steep hills along the river bank left no room for baggage. Clothes and tents rotted in the rain. The salty river water was almost undrinkable. Nerves were as frayed as the clothing the party wore. One rainy, windy day Clark wrote that Sacagawea was displeased with him. He chose not to say why.[6]

◈Pacific Ocean in Sight◈

Convinced that they could not reach the ocean by boat, first Lewis and then Clark hiked to the coast. Each was accompanied by a small party of men. With Clark went York and Charbonneau. Standing on a high point, Clark's group regarded the waves dashing against the rocks and the immense ocean with astonishment.[7]

The Chinook speakers had been much in evidence since the expedition first reached the Columbia. They smoked with the Corps and enjoyed the music and festivities. As the explorers neared the coast, more Chinooks came to see them. Lewis and Clark traded with them, but considered their prices too high. The captains also came to distrust the native people, because some Chinooks stole from the Corps when they could.[8] Chinooks, however, did not consider thefts from the Corps to be stealing, since Lewis and Clark were not Chinook.

Clark returned to camp after his visit to the ocean and found Lewis trying to purchase a robe of sea otter skin from one of the Chinooks. The man refused red beads and white beads, a blanket, and even Clark's watch. At her waist, Sacagawea wore a belt of blue beads—these were chief beads, highly prized by all the coast Native Americans.[9] To make the trade, Sacagawea gave up her belt. In return, the captains gave her a coat of blue cloth.

◈Where to Camp for the Winter?◈

The expedition needed a winter campsite. The mountain snows—twenty feet deep or more in the Rockies—and frozen river water made the return journey back toward the East impossible until at least the first of April. Besides, American and British ships cruised the Pacific Coast, trading with Native Americans. Lewis and Clark hoped to contact one of these trading vessels and make the trip home by sea. Thomas Jefferson had given them a letter of credit to pay their way.

The miserable weather along the north side of the Columbia (now Washington State), did not let up. Game was scarce. They had heard elk were plentiful on the south side of the river in present-day Oregon. Should they go there? In a rare move for explorers, Lewis and Clark put the matter to a vote.[10] Sacagawea spoke up for a place where there were plenty of "Pota"—that is, potatoes or wapato roots. Relating this incident in his journal, Clark referred to Sacagawea for the first time as "Janey," the nickname he probably had given her.[11]

Like Sacagawea, the majority of the party voted for the south side of the Columbia. The Corps crossed the river, and Meriwether Lewis struck out on foot to find a site. For some time now, the party's diet had consisted of pounded fish boiled in a little salt water. This made many of the men, including Clark, ill. Sacagawea renewed his spirits. She had made some bread and carefully kept it for little Baptiste, but the bread became wet and sour. She offered it to Clark, who ate it with great satisfaction. This was the only bread he had had in months. Finally, some of the men had luck hunting elk—the first taken since crossing the Rocky Mountains. After eating the bone marrow, Sacagawea chopped up the shank bones, boiled them, and made grease.[12] Grease like this was used for oiling guns and boots.

❖Setting up Camp❖

Lewis returned to camp with good news: He had found a place for winter quarters on a small river about seven miles inland from the ocean. Throughout December 1805, slowed by snow and hail, the Corps built eight cabins enclosed by a stockade. By Christmas Eve, the fort was livable. Sacagawea, Baptiste, and Charbonneau shared a room, as did Lewis and Clark. The other members of the Corps and various supplies took the remaining rooms. In honor of the friendly natives living nearby, they named their new home Fort Clatsop.

On Christmas morning, the men celebrated by waking the captains at dawn with a volley of gunshots,

— ❖ —

This replica of Fort Clatsop, where the Corps spent the winter of 1805–1806 near the Pacific Ocean, was reconstructed from William Clark's floor plan. The nearby Clatsop tribe was friendly and visited often. Still, from dusk till dawn the gates of the fort were shut, and a sentinel was always posted.

shouts, and singing. As usual, the day was damp. (During the four months the Corps lived at Fort Clatsop, only twelve days were without rain. Six of those were overcast.) Christmas dinner was spoiled elk, fish, a few roots, and water. Still, the group exchanged gifts. Sacagawea gave William Clark two dozen white weasel (ermine) tails. This was a gift highly prized by the Shoshones, who used them to decorate their short coats.[13]

At the first of the year a few men of the Corps went to the ocean to make salt from the ocean water. They returned to the fort with blubber given to them by their Clatsop neighbors. They had taken it from a beached whale. When cooked, the blubber was tasty. Right away, Clark decided to take a party of men to the coast and get more of it. Hearing this, Sacagawea asked to go, too. She had, she said, traveled a long way with the expedition to see the great waters. Now that a monstrous fish was to be seen as well, she thought it very hard that she could not be permitted to see either one of them.[14] (Scientists had, by 1806, classified whales as mammals, but this was not widely known.) When William Clark set out after an early breakfast on January 6, 1806, Sacagawea and Charbonneau were with his party.

By the time the group reached the whale, one of the Pacific Coast tribes had stripped it of flesh and blubber. Clark measured the skeleton at about 92 meters (100 feet). From the Tillamook tribe, Clark purchased 136 kilograms (300 pounds) of blubber and some oil. The only record historians have of Sacagawea's reaction to the whale comes from Shoshone oral tradition. In later years, the story goes, when she told her people the size of the monstrous fish, they would not believe her. According to the Shoshone stories, Sacagawea also saw seals while in the vicinity of the Pacific and considered them an odd race of humans. When she tried to talk to them, they disappeared into the water. The Shoshones did believe Sacagawea's account of these slippery people. They, too, had seen seals on trips to the Columbia River.[15]

◈Surviving the Winter◈

The Corps survived the dismal winter by keeping busy. With Sacagawea's help, the men dressed skins to replace their rotting shirts and moccasins.[16] They repaired their weapons and canoes and carried on a steady relationship with the Clatsops and the Clatsop chief, Yanakasac Coboway. Lewis and Clark worked on their journals. They had not had so much time to write since leaving Fort Mandan! Using notes and sketches he had made, Clark finished his maps of land and river routes from the Mandan villages to the coast. Lewis classified trees, shrubs, ferns, and fish. He also wrote detailed accounts of Native American dress, customs, tools, and canoes.

The original plan was to leave the coast in April 1806, but as early as mid-March the explorers noticed signs of spring. At once they began preparing for the long journey home. Since the captains had not seen or heard of a trading vessel in the area, they had given up hope of returning by ship. Actually though, an American ship was in the vicinity. For several weeks in November, the ship had cruised the mouth of the Columbia, trading with Native Americans for furs. No word of the ship reached the explorers, however.

Lewis and Clark knew the Nez Perces—who were holding the Corps' horses for them—would move east of the Rocky Mountains once the snow in higher elevations melted. In addition, the captains were anxious to investigate new trails Sacagawea's people had described to them and to explore the Yellowstone River.[17] They had a problem, though. The three canoes at hand left them short of boats. Their trade goods were low—about enough to fill two handkerchiefs, Lewis observed.[18] With Lewis's gold-laced officer's coat, they purchased one canoe. Another they simply stole from the Clatsops. The boat was unattended. Besides, they told themselves, over the winter the Clatsops had stolen six elk from them.[19] The boat would do as payment.

For his kindness, the explorers gave Chief Coboway the fort, its furnishings, and a certificate of thanks. They also gave the Clatsops a message for any sea traders who arrived in the area after their departure. They had made it across the North American continent to the Pacific Ocean and wanted people to know about their accomplishment if something should happened to the Corps on the way home. To the Chinook chief, they gave a certificate of kindness similar to the one they gave Chief Coboway. During frequent visits to the fort, both chiefs had given the Corps valuable information about other Native Americans on the coast.

❖The Journey Back Begins❖

Finally, on March 23, 1806, the canoes were loaded and launched. The last four months had been hard to endure but, Clark wrote, they had lived as well as they had any right to expect.[20] That Sunday afternoon, the Corps, along with Sacagawea, Charbonneau, and Baptiste, left the Pacific Coast just as they had found it—in the blowing wind and rain.

RETURN TO FORT MANDAN

Sacagawea and the Corps of Discovery started east from Fort Clatsop in the spring of 1806. Swollen with thawing ice and snow, the water of the Columbia ran high—and the Corps had to paddle against the current. The party faced other troubles. As the expedition portaged the lower Cascades of the Columbia—in the pouring rain—the Chinooks watching their progress threw stones and shouted insults.

◈Close Call for Seaman◈

Even worse, several members of the tribe attempted to "dognap" Seaman. Lewis's big, black Newfoundland had been a real help and companion to the Corps. The dog had guarded the Corps against grizzlies. He had warned of a charging buffalo. The dognappers were taking Seaman toward a nearby village. Alerted to this by helpful Native Americans, Captain Lewis sent three men to the dog's rescue, with orders to shoot, if necessary. The party met no resistance, and Seaman soon was back in camp with the Corps.[1]

Unlike the villains—as Lewis called them—who tried to take Seaman, many Native Americans the expedition encountered along the Columbia River were friendly and honest. The chief of one village, mortified that Seaman had been threatened, apologized to Lewis and Clark. The thieves were just a few bad men, the chief assured the captains. His nation had no wish to displease the Corps.[2]

To cross the Celilo Falls and continue its journey by land, the Corps needed horses. In exchange for them, Lewis and Clark traded their canoes and medical skills. The Corps reached the top of the falls on April 19, 1806, just as the salmon run began. From the Celilo Falls, the expedition wound its way up the Columbia River. The two canoes left untraded were in the water, tended by a few men. Sacagawea and the others traveled the shore with the baggage-laden horses. One month after leaving the Pacific Coast, the expedition reached the mouth of the Walla Walla River. The principal chief of the Walla Walla, Yellept,

— ❖ —

Sacagawea and the Corps left Fort Clatsop in the spring of 1806. On the way back east, they transported their canoes and supplies around the Celilo Falls, reaching the top just as the salmon run began. In this mural painted for the Oregon State Capitol Building, Sacagawea is on the far right.

still had the peace medal Lewis and Clark had given him the previous October.

❖ Life Among the Walla Wallas ❖

Chief Yellept greeted the party warmly. A Shoshone captive lived among the Walla Wallas. Through this woman, Sacagawea translated for the Corps. Chief Yellept urged Lewis and Clark to remain in the area for a while. Yellept wanted the explorers to meet his people and their neighbors. Though in a hurry to get home, the captains agreed. Chief Yellept presented Lewis and Clark with firewood and roasted fish. He gave William Clark an elegant white horse. In return, Clark gave Yellept his sword. Many Walla Wallas needed medical attention. Clark set one man's broken arm, eased another's knee pain, and treated sore eyes. That night, the Walla Wallas and their neighbors—more than three hundred men, women, and children—joined the explorers in dancing to the fiddle music of Pierre Cruzatte.[3]

The next morning, Chief Yellept furnished the Corps with canoes for crossing the Columbia. On April 30, 1806, Sacagawea and the Corps of Discovery left the Walla Wallas and headed toward the land of the Nez Perce. All during April, the weather had been frigid, with heavy white frosts and snow on the hilltops. Still, from a distance, the unfurling leaves of the cottonwood trees appeared green. The birds were singing. Conditions seemed right for proceeding on. The Corps already had been traveling a few days when three young Walla Walla men caught up with them. The trio wished to return a steel trap one of the white men had left behind. These Native Americans were, Lewis and Clark wrote, the most hospitable, honest, and sincere people they had met during their voyage.[4]

On the return trip to Fort Mandan, Lewis and Clark planned to save time by traveling overland rather than fighting the waters of the Snake and Clearwater as they had done on the westbound journey. That is why when they reached the Snake, they crossed it and traveled up the north bank. At the Clearwater, they did the same. Back in Nez Perce country, they found Chief Twisted Hair had kept their horses for them, as promised. Twisted Hair had even saved their saddles in a flood.

❖Back Among the Nez Perce❖

Most of the Nez Perces were as hospitable now as they had been in the autumn of 1805. Sacagawea and other interpreters helped the captains communicate during a council. The council took place in a lodge made of leather that the tribe provided. Because the captains' English had to be translated through three languages in addition to Sacagawea's Shoshone, the council took half the day. Among other things, Lewis and Clark spoke of the wish of the United States Government to restore peace and harmony among Native Americans. One young Nez Perce man—the son of a chief recently killed in battle—told the captains their words gladdened his heart. The youth presented them with a fine mare and colt in token of his determination to follow their advice.[5]

The Nez Perces warned the Corps against attempting to cross the Bitterroots of the Rockies too early in the spring. The snow in the mountains was still much too deep to allow safe travel over the Lolo Trail. They told the explorers about a good camping place just across the Clearwater River. The Corps could stay there until the snow on the mountains melted. The Nez Perces even offered a canoe for the Corps to use in transporting its baggage across the river. Following the advice of these Native Americans, on May 14, 1806, the Corps set up Camp Chopunnish on the Clearwater, near modern-day Kamiah, Idaho.

❖Waiting for Warmer Weather❖

As they waited for warmer weather at Camp Chopunnish, the captains continued their studies of the land and Native American culture. They also doctored the local people. The members of the Corps and the Nez Perces danced together, had foot and horse races, and played games. Food was alarmingly scarce, however. The men continued to trade for horses and dogs to eat, while Sacagawea gathered fennel roots and stored them for the trip across the Rocky Mountains. That crossing, Lewis wrote, was the wretched part of the journey. Not one of the party had forgotten its suffering there the previous September (1805). He doubted they ever would.[6]

❖Sacagawea's Baby Gets Sick❖

While the explorers were camped at Chopunnish, Baptiste fell dangerously ill. The baby's fever was high, his neck and throat swollen. He was cutting teeth. The two captains gave the boy cream of tartar and sulfur flour and applied a poultice of boiled onions to his neck. This treatment they continued on a regular basis. The baby's neck continued to swell. Baptiste's condition remained serious for over two weeks. At last, the captains could pronounce him nearly well. Today, historians believe Sacagawea's little boy may have had mumps or tonsillitis.[7]

◆Setting Out Again◆

Despite the advice of the Nez Perces, the Corps was impatient to cross the Rocky Mountains. Lewis and Clark wanted to reach the Mandan and Hidatsa villages before the Missouri River froze. If they did not arrive there in good time, snow and ice would force them to delay another winter before returning downriver to St. Louis. On June 10, 1806, the Corps left Camp Chopunnish. By the middle of the month, the party was heading up the Lolo Trail into the Bitterroot Mountains. Two days later, they crossed the rapid, cold water of Hungry Creek, where Clark and his hunters had once tied up horse meat for Captain Lewis and his starving men. Within a few miles they found themselves in snow twelve to fifteen feet deep. Snow shrouded the pines. The June air was frigid, numbing their hands and feet. The horses, the scientific records the explorers had kept, the Corps itself—all faced grave danger if they proceeded on.

◆Turning Back◆

Dejected, the Corps turned back toward Hungry Creek. This was the first time its members had been compelled to retreat. To add insult to injury, as they camped that evening, the sky pelted them with rain. At Hungry Creek, Sacagawea gathered a quantity of tasty, early-blooming plants. Although Shoshones used it for food, the plant was unknown to science at the time. Meriwether Lewis added it to his collection. Today, the plant Sacagawea gave him is recognized as western spring beauty.[8]

❖On Course Again❖

Within the week, the Corps approached the mountains again, accompanied now by Nez Perce guides. The snow had melted to a manageable depth of about seven feet. The Corps retrieved the baggage it had left alongside the trail and plodded through the snowy mountains. The Nez Perces, Captain Lewis wrote, were admirable pilots, always capable of finding the trail.[9]

On June 29, 1806, Sacagawea, Baptiste, and the men of the Corps bid the snow farewell. Crossing into modern-day Missoula County, Montana, they camped at the Lolo Hot Springs. This was an opportunity to bathe. The Nez Perces enjoyed soaking in the steaming hot water, then running and jumping in the ice-cold creek. The following day, the Corps reached its old camp at Travelers Rest. The trip across the Bitterroots had taken six days—half the time required during the fall of 1805. For leading the Corps safely across the Rockies, the Nez Perce guides received two rifles.

At Travelers Rest, the explorers refreshed themselves and put their weapons in order. Something new was about to happen. While on the Pacific Coast, the captains had decided to split up the Corps and venture into territory left unexplored on the way west. From Travelers Rest, Captain Lewis would go north, investigate the Marias River, and determine if it offered a route to the rich fur country of Canada. William Clark would head overland to Camp Fortunate (where the expedition had hidden its canoes and baggage the previous August, 1805). From Camp Fortunate, Clark's party would continue to the Three Forks of the Missouri, then travel east and explore the Yellowstone River.

◈Lewis and Clark Split Up◈

On July 3, 1806, Meriwether Lewis rode north with nine men. That same day, Sacagawea and her family (as well as York, Seaman, and the remaining members of the Corps) started south with Clark, taking with them the fifty horses the Corps now owned. The captains planned to reunite at the junction of the Yellowstone and Missouri rivers.

A few days after starting out without Lewis, Clark's party reached a broad level plain where the trail scattered in many directions. Which way to go? Because she was in the land of her childhood, Sacagawea was able to tell Captain Clark that she recognized the plain: She had been here many times with her Shoshone people gathering camas. From a high part of the plain, she said, they would discover a pass in the mountains beyond which lay the canoes hidden at Camp Fortunate. They went that way. Ascending a small rise, Sacagawea pointed to the gap through which they should pass. Clark's notes for that day and the comments he added just one week later suggest he took Sacagawea's words seriously.[10] In just two days, Clark's party reached the old camp. They found the canoes and supplies they had left there in good condition.

◆Sacagawea Offers Advice◆

After spending one night in camp, the Corps started by horse and canoe toward its next destination: the Three Forks of the Missouri. Once there, Sacagawea offered Clark advice on the best route through the mountain passes to the Yellowstone River. In his journal, William Clark wrote that Sacagawea had been of great service to him as a pilot through this country. She recommended the gap to the south; that was the one he would take.[11] Today, the pass Sacagawea recommended is known as Bozeman Pass. On July 15, 1806, she, Clark, and the eleven others in the party reached the Yellowstone, having traveled almost fifty miles in two days.

Trouble plagued them. The plains were beautiful—and level—but the stony ground injured the feet of the horses. When Charbonneau rode out after a buffalo, his horse threw him. Yet another man fell from his horse and punctured his thigh. Maybe, Clark thought, they should continue this trip by water. For the next week, they remained at Canoe Camp on the north side of the Yellowstone, making clothes and building new boats. The new canoes were necessary because, at Three Forks, Clark had sent several men down the Missouri in the old ones to join Captain Lewis.

◆Horses Disappear◆

One morning, Clark's group woke to some excitement: twenty-four of their fifty horses had disappeared—stolen by several Crow bands, Clark thought, for this was Crow country.[12] By July 24, 1806, the Corps had built the new boats and were ready to put the boats in the river. Sacagawea and her family traveled down the Yellowstone with Clark. In the meantime, Sergeant Nathaniel Pryor and three men started with the remaining horses overland to the Mandan villages.

The swift river took Clark's party seventy miles the first day. On their journey, the abundance of elk, buffalo, and wolves was so incredible, Clark wrote, that he was just going to quit mentioning it.[13] Late the following afternoon, he and the others saw another remarkable sight. Not far from the river bank, a butte, a hill with sloping sides and a flat top, rose almost two hundred feet above the plain. The captain decided to climb it. Standing atop the butte, he saw the snowy Rocky Mountains—and immense herds of elk, buffalo, and wolves. Native Americans had carved figures on the face of the rock. Clark added his name and the date: July 25, 1806. He named the place Pompy's Tower, for little Baptiste, whom Clark had nicknamed Pomp. (Located near present Billings, Montana, the butte is commonly called Pompey's Pillar.) Two days later, Clark's party had its last view of the Rockies which had been in sight now for almost three months.[14]

❖Down the Yellowstone River❖

The Corps made its way down the Yellowstone, stopped sometimes by great herds of buffalo crossing the river.

More troublesome were the mosquitoes that tormented the party as it approached the junction of the Yellowstone and Missouri rivers. Everyone was up at dawn on August 3, 1806. Who could sleep with mosquitoes buzzing and biting them? They continued on and in a few hours reached the Corps campsite of the previous year, in present-day McKenzie County, North Dakota. Here mosquitoes were ferociously thick. Preparing the skins the party desperately needed for clothes was impossible. Seaman, although in a tent,

— ◈ —

The expedition made its way down the Yellowstone, stopped from time to time by buffalo crossing the river. Karl Bodmer's painting shows a great herd coming from the high prairie to drink. On the far left, a stag guards a gang of elk.

was bitten so often, he howled with pain. Little Baptiste's face was pink and swollen.[15]

This was where they were to meet Captain Lewis, but conditions were intolerable. Clark left Lewis a note stuck on a pole and led his party on downriver. The next campsite was even worse. Sacagawea battled mosquitoes for several more days. Finally, rain and a hard blowing wind left the air clear, cold, and free of insects.

The party's joy turned to surprise early the next morning. Sergeant Pryor and his men came downriver in two bullboats. Some of the Crow had slipped off with the rest of the Corps horses, Sergeant Pryor explained. Remembering the round boats made by the Mandans and Hidatsas of wood hoops and buffalo skin, Pryor and his men had fashioned two similar tubs and started downriver. The bullboats had ridden the rapids beautifully. At the mouth of the Yellowstone, the men had found Clark's message to Captain Lewis. Assuming Lewis already had found it and proceeded on, Pryor had taken the note from the pole and brought it with him.

Captain Clark was not too concerned about the waylaid message. He felt confident that Lewis would see signs of the water party as it traveled down the river. Eventually, Lewis would catch up. What Clark did not know was that over one week earlier, Meriwether Lewis had been involved in a bloody skirmish with a party of Blackfeet.

Clark and company loaded the canoes—and the two bullboats—and proceeded on, expecting Captain Lewis to show up soon. As the party came closer to the vicinity of the Mandan and Hidatsa villages, Sacagawea presented Clark with more gifts—a large, crimson gooseberry and some golden currants.[16]

❖Lewis is Wounded❖

Three days later, on August 12, 1806, they were heading down the present Little Knife River in North Dakota when the white pirogue came into sight. Where was Captain Lewis? Alarmed, Clark boarded the boat and found the captain seriously wounded. Not from Blackfeet, however. Lewis and Pierre Cruzatte (the fiddle player) had been out hunting after the fight with the Blackfeet when Cruzatte accidentally shot Lewis in the buttocks. Cruzatte had mistaken his captain, who wore brown leather, for an elk!

Backing up and relating the details of the fight with the Native Americans, Lewis explained that one of the Blackfeet had attempted to steal a rifle belonging to the Corps. In the following scuffle, one of Lewis's men had stabbed the Blackfoot, who had then fled, fallen to the ground, and died. In the meantime, Lewis had awakened to find his gun missing. He had drawn his pistol, given warning, then shot a Blackfoot warrior who was stealing his horse. Certain of pursuit, Lewis and his men had ridden over one hundred miles in the next twenty-four hours.[17]

❖Lewis and Clark Reunite❖

Although Lewis insisted now that he was fine, the wound he had received at the hand of the near-sighted Cruzatte was serious and so painful Lewis was forced to remain in the pirogue, even at night. Even writing was difficult. On the day the captain overtook Clark, he made just a few notes in his journal. Then he left its continuation to his friend until he recovered. In fact, Lewis never wrote in the journals again.[18] Two days after this reunion, on August 14, 1806, Sacagawea and the Corps reached the villages of the Mandans and Hidatsas. Within the week, Lewis and Clark canoed down the Missouri to St. Louis and into history. Sacagawea's journey with the Lewis and Clark Expedition had come to an end. Her ties with William Clark, however, had not.

FAREWELL

Sacagawea's story has two endings. Both stories, however, begin the same way. The Corps of Discovery arrived back in the vicinity of the Mandan and Hidatsa villages in the middle of August 1806. For the next few days, Clark concentrated on the main business of the party. Lewis was still weak and in pain from the gunshot wound he had suffered at the hands of fellow elk hunter, Pierre Cruzatte.

One of Captain Clark's first goals was to invite Native American leaders together to convince someone to accompany him and Lewis to the United States to meet President Thomas

Jefferson. The Hidatsas refused. They were involved in tribal wars and afraid of the Sioux the Corps would have to pass on the trip downriver to St. Louis. (Also, one chief among the Arikaras had already gone to Washington and not been seen since.)

❖On to Meet the President❖

Eventually, Sheheke (Chief Big White) of the Mandans agreed to accompany the captains to Washington, but only if he could take his wife and son. The captains agreed. It was eventually decided that René Jusseaume, the French interpreter employed by Lewis and Clark in the winter of 1804–1805, should accompany them, too. With these details ironed out, the expedition moved downriver. On Saturday, August 17, 1806, the Hidatsas and the explorers said goodbye. At some time, too, Sacagawea and her family told the captains goodbye. For now, at least, the Charbonneaus were to remain at the villages.

❖Sacagawea Stays Behind❖

According to William Clark's journal, Toussaint Charbonneau wanted very much to accompany the expedition to see President Jefferson as an interpreter with the Hidatsas. Because the Hidatsas refused to accompany the crew downriver, however, Charbonneau was discharged and paid. For services rendered to the expedition, Charbonneau received five hundred dollars. This included the price of a horse and the tipi the Charbonneaus and the captains had shared on the trip west. Clark's journal entry did not mention any payment for Sacagawea.

In writing of these events, William Clark noted that he and Lewis had offered Charbonneau transport to Illinois. Charbonneau had refused the offer. He did not know anyone there, he said. He would have no way to make a living. Then Clark had offered to take Jean Baptiste—now nineteen months old and a beautiful, promising child, Clark wrote—and raise him. According to Clark, both Sacagawea and Charbonneau were willing to allow this, but considered Baptiste too young. In one year, they suggested, Baptiste would be old enough to leave Sacagawea. Charbonneau would then take Baptiste to Clark if Clark would be so friendly as to raise the boy in such a manner as Clark thought proper. To this, the captain had agreed.[1]

The expedition—faces bearded, buckskins tattered from the rigors of the expedition—finally got underway. Just one man, Private John Colter, was absent from the departing group. Private Colter asked Lewis and Clark for permission to go with two traders into fur country, and his discharge was granted.

The men left the Hidatsas and started down the Missouri to St. Louis, stopping briefly to pick up Mandan Chief Sheheke and his family. After the chief's tearful parting with relatives and friends, everyone was ready to go. For the most part, the trip to St. Louis was uneventful. The party did hear daunting news. Traders they passed traveling upriver told them nothing had been heard of the expedition once it left the Mandan villages in 1805. Most people in the United States either had given its members up for lost or dead or forgotten about them completely. President Thomas Jefferson, though, still held out hope of their survival.

The Corps of Discovery had a little trouble with warring Sioux. Sure enough, the Sioux taunted the Corps as it went downriver, daring the white men to come ashore. Insults were exchanged. The Corps kept to the Missouri. Slowly but surely, Captain Lewis's wound healed. At noon on September 23, 1806, the victorious river party landed in St. Louis, having saluted the town with a round of shots. The crowd lining the riverfront cheered. Two days later some of the people of St. Louis honored the men with a dinner and ball. Eighteen toasts were drunk, the first for Thomas Jefferson. The last toast went like this: to "Captains Lewis and Clark—Their perilous services endear them to every American heart."[2]

Meriwether Lewis's last note in his journal had come six weeks earlier, just before he handed the journals over to his cocaptain. In extreme pain from his fresh gunshot wound, Lewis had summoned the effort to make a final botanical entry. It had concerned the pin cherry. On the morning following the party and toasts in St. Louis, William Clark took up his pen and noted simply: "a fine morning we commenced wrighting &c."[3] By this, Clark meant that they began writing "and so on." This note made by him was the last of the daily journal entries.

◈What Became of the Others?◈

No one knows where Sacagawea was at this time. It is probable that she, Baptiste, and Charbonneau remained in the vicinity of the Mandan and Hidatsa villages. Other members of the expedition scattered. Some of the men became farmers; others reenlisted in the army. Several, like John Colter, returned to the wilderness. Colter became the first known white American to penetrate the wilderness of modern-day Yellowstone Park.[4] Pierre Cruzatte, the near-sighted hunter and musician, was killed by the Blackfeet. York remained William Clark's slave for a time. Eventually, however, Clark gave York his freedom, along with a team of horses and a wagon. With these, York set up a freight-hauling business.[5] As for Seaman, after the expedition the lively grizzly-chaser simply disappeared from recorded history.

◈Lewis Dies◈

Lewis had turned thirty-one while the Corps of Discovery was camped near Sacagawea's people

(August 18, 1805) on the outbound journey. On that day, Captain Lewis wrote in his journal that although in all likelihood he had lived about half his life, he had done very little for humankind. He was determined to do more.[6] Only three years after returning to the United States in glory, however, Meriwether Lewis died. Following the expedition, he was appointed governor of the Louisiana Territory. This was an honor, but Lewis, as a scientist and explorer, probably was not happy tending business. Then some of his expenses as governor were questioned. Among these was a charge of five hundred dollars to help return Chief Sheheke to his people. Outraged, Lewis set out for Washington, D.C., with papers backing up his requests. On the evening of October 10, 1809, he stopped at a resting place for travelers in the Tennessee wilderness. Late that night, he stumbled from his cabin, shot in the side and head. At daybreak the following morning, lying alone beside the trail, Meriwether Lewis died from his self-inflicted wounds. He was thirty-five.

Some people once thought Lewis might have been robbed and murdered. Today, however, most leading historians believe he killed himself. Besides his troubles as an administrator, he was unlucky in love and facing bankruptcy. Since returning from the expedition, he had been drinking heavily. To his disappointment, the expedition journals had not been published.

❖Clark Settles in St. Louis❖

After the expedition, Clark settled in St. Louis, where he served as Brigadier General of the militia for the Louisiana Territory. He was also appointed Superintendent of Indian Affairs for the vast region of the American West. Clark tried to treat Native Americans fairly. They, in turn, liked him, and nicknamed him Chief Red Hair. Eventually, he was named Governor of the Missouri Territory. Throughout Clark's life, the untimely death of his partner in discovery troubled him deeply; he named his first son Meriwether Lewis Clark. When William Clark died in 1838, crowds of admirers attended his funeral. He was sixty-eight.

The Lewis and Clark Expedition was a tremendous success. With important contributions from Sacagawea, Meriwether Lewis and William Clark blazed a trail into uncharted land and returned with a wealth of information. The captains kept journals as they traveled that overflowed with their discoveries. Fruits, flowers, trees—Lewis and Clark described almost two hundred in all, some of them brought to their attention by Sacagawea. Coyotes, porcupines, prairie dogs: their writings note more than one hundred animals previously unknown to science. They introduced their curious fellow Americans to the West, describing a country that until the expedition had been a mystery. There were neither fantastic mountains of salt there nor mysterious, lost tribes descended from the Welsh. There were, however, snow-capped mountains, gorges, and rivers, and an extensive Native American population.

◈The Journals◈

The journals showed that contrary to popular belief, Native Americans were not savages, but people of honor who like Sacagawea, shared food, advice, and knowledge of the land. The journals of the Lewis and Clark Expedition contain the captains' extensive observations on Native American culture: clothing, customs, religion, vocabularies, and more. They offer the first written description of the Nez Perces, Shoshones, Flatheads, and other Native Americans.

Lewis and Clark did not discover a direct water route across the continent. Still, in a letter to President Jefferson, Meriwether Lewis could write that they had discovered the most practical route that existed across the country. By water and land—not by water alone—it was possible to reach the Pacific Ocean. Not only that, the land was rich in beaver and otter. The land of the Louisiana Purchase was a fur trapper's dream.[7]

◈What Became of Sacagawea?◈

What became of Sacagawea, Charbonneau, and Jean Baptiste? As Clark's fortunes rose in St. Louis, he remembered Sacagawea and his offer to raise her son. In the days just following the Corps departure from the Mandan and Hidatsa villages, in fact, the matter had weighed on his mind. In a letter written to Toussaint Charbonneau (August 20, 1806) just a few days after leaving the Hidatsa villages, Clark expressed his concern for the Charbonneaus. Sacagawea, he noted, had been on the dangerous and fatiguing journey to the Pacific and back and deserved a greater reward than that which they (he and Meriwether Lewis) had had in their power to give her at the Mandans.

"As to your little son (my boy Pomp)," Clark wrote, "you well know my fondness for him and my anxiety to take and raise him as my own child." Clark went on to offer Charbonneau a variety of opportunities. If, Clark said, Charbonneau decided to bring Baptiste to St. Louis, Janey (Clark's nickname for Sacagawea) should come, too, to care for the boy until Clark could meet the child. The captain wished the family great success and closed the letter: " . . . with anxious expectations of seeing my little dancing boy, Baptiste, I shall remain your friend. William Clark."[8]

It is almost certain that a few months after the end of the expedition, Sacagawea and her family moved downriver to St. Louis. It is definitely true that Clark took Baptiste into his care and provided his education. After this point, however, Sacagawea's story blurs. What historians have from written records is this: In the fall of 1810, Toussaint Charbonneau purchased

had no acquaintance or prospects of making
a living below, and must continue to live in the
way that he had done. I offered to take his [10]
little son a butifull promising child who is
19 months old to which they both himself & wife
wer willing provided the child had been
weaned. they observed that in one year the boy
would be sufficiently old to leave his mother &
he would then take him to me if I would be
so friendly as to raise the child for him in
such a manner as I thought proper, to which
I agreed &. — we droped down to the Big white
Chiefs Mandan Village ½ a mile below on the
South Side, all the Indians proceeded on down
by land. and I walked to the lodge of the Chief
whome I found sorrounded by his friends
the men were setting in a circle smokeing
and the womin Crying. he sent his baggage
with his wife & son, with the Interpreter
Jessonme & his wife and 2 children to the
Canoes provided for them. after smokeing
one pipe, and distributeing some powder &
lead which we had given him. he informed
me that he was ready and we were accomp

— ❖ —

William Clark's journal entry of August 17, 1806, related his offer to Sacagawea to take and raise her son, Baptiste. At the time, Sacagawea and her husband considered the boy too young to leave his mother.

some land from Clark, but sold the land back to him the following spring. This was just as a new expedition was preparing to set out upriver from St. Louis. Seeking the fur trade, the expedition was led not by Clark, but a man named Henry Brackenridge.

In his journal entry dated April 11, 1811, Brackenridge wrote that when leaving St. Louis this expedition had on board a Frenchman—Toussaint Charbonneau—and his wife. Both had accompanied Lewis and Clark to the Pacific. Both had been of great service. Brackenridge described the woman as good, mild, and gentle. She was ill, however, and longed to revisit her country. Charbonneau, too, was weary of civilized life.[9]

The confusion with Brackenridge's journal entry comes because Brackenridge referred to the young Native American woman traveling with Charbonneau not by name, but simply as his wife. She was, Brackenridge said, a woman of the Snake nation. Charbonneau had several Shoshone wives. Some writers, especially in the past, who wish to take Sacagawea's life in a different direction have pointed out that Brackenridge could have mistaken one of these other Shoshone wives for Sacagawea. Today, though, most historians accept Brackenridge's belief that the young woman with Charbonneau truly was Sacagawea.

From here, the trail becomes even less clear. In the spring of 1811, another expedition besides

Brackenridge's left St. Louis. Its purpose was to build a fort on the banks of the Missouri River in present-day South Dakota (just below the North Dakota border). Fort Manuel was completed in November 1811. Serving as clerk at the fort was a former businessman named John C. Luttig. In his journal, Luttig recorded daily business and activities. His journal states that Toussaint Charbonneau spent some time at Fort Manuel. The journal says also that on December 20, 1812, Charbonneau's wife died there of a fever. She was, Luttig wrote, the best woman in the fort and about twenty-five years old. If only John Luttig had noted the dead woman's name! He, like Henry Brackenridge, identified her simply as Charbonneau's wife, and a Snake (Shoshone).[10] There is no proof that she was Sacagawea. That is one reason Sacagawea's story now leads in another direction. It is a story based on Shoshone oral tradition.

❖Shoshone Oral Tradition❖

According to this tradition, Sacagawea lived to an old age and died revered by her people on the Wind River Reservation in present-day Wyoming. What happened, the Shoshones say, is this: Following the Lewis and Clark Expedition, Sacagawea argued with Charbonneau, left him, and became a wanderer. She lived with the Comanches for a time. Once back with the Shoshones, she was reunited with her son, Baptiste, and with the nephew she had adopted while traveling west. The nephew related to her and Chief Cameahwait was named Bazil. These details and others were recorded by researchers into Sacagawea's life who became increasingly curious about her as the importance of the Lewis and Clark Expedition was realized.

◈Sacagawea's Legacy◈

Some people interviewed said they had personally known the Sacagawea who lived on the Wind River Reservation. For example, sixty years after John Luttig noted his belief that Sacagawea died at Fort Manuel in 1811, an agricultural agent at Wind River said he met Sacagawea on the reservation in 1871. This Shoshone woman spoke both French and English. She told of being captured by the Hidatsas as a girl and of going on the journey west. She described the big fish she had seen on the Pacific beach and spoke of other incidents related to the expedition.[11]

This Sacagawea, the Shoshones said, had a great impact on their people, influencing them to adapt to the ways of the white people and learn to farm. She lived to be almost one hundred years old. On April 9, 1884, she died and was buried at Wind River. Laid to rest with her within a few years were the two men known on the reservation as Baptiste and Bazil. Almost eighty years later (1963), the Wyoming branch of the Daughters of the American Revolution erected a stone at the site. It recognizes the woman buried

— ⬦ —

As a sixteen-year-old Shoshone woman, Sacagawea and her infant son accompanied Meriwether Lewis and William Clark from present-day North Dakota to the Pacific Ocean and back. Frederic Remington's Lewis and Clark on the Columbia *depicts the two explorers dressed in Revolutionary War uniforms rather than the buckskins they usually wore. Standing in the background are Sacagawea and her family.*

there as Sacagawea, a guide with the Lewis and Clark Expedition, 1805–1806.[12]

No one knows beyond the shadow of a doubt whether this woman was the true Sacagawea. In the end, this is not what is most important. In 1805–1806, a sixteen-year-old Shoshone woman and her infant son accompanied Meriwether Lewis and William Clark from the Mandan villages of present-day North Dakota to the Pacific Ocean and back. As the Corps of Discovery traveled and worked, Sacagawea cared for Baptiste and helped the men by sharing with them the nutritious food she gathered. She probably also helped them sew much-needed moccasins and repaired their ragged clothes. Her presence calmed the Native Americans that the armed and bearded strangers encountered as they explored a land that was to them wilderness. From her Shoshone brother, Chief Cameahwait, she helped the captains purchase the horses that eventually carried the Corps across the mountains of the Rockies. On at least two occasions during the return trip, when Clark was in a hurry to reach the Mandan villages before the Missouri River froze, she piloted the captain across what was to him unfamiliar terrain.

Not once in the journals do either Lewis or Clark record any regret at having a teenage woman and her baby as part of the expedition. Their writings present her as calm, courageous, and uncomplaining. This, despite her illness during the difficult crossing of the

Great Falls of the Missouri and Baptiste's illness later at Camp Chopunnish. In fact, one of the few personal comments comes in the journals when Captain Clark states that Sacagawea is displeased with him.

Regardless of whether Sacagawea died in South Dakota as a young woman or old and highly regarded at the Wind River Reservation in Wyoming, the truth remains that in 1805–1806 she was a vital member of the groundbreaking Corps of Discovery. For that, she is honored.

CHRONOLOGY

1789 ❖ Sacagawea is born to Shoshone parents in present-day Idaho.

1801 ❖ Sacagawea is captured around age twelve by Hidatsa warriors and taken to their village in present-day North Dakota.

1803 ❖ **December 20**: United States purchases Louisiana Territory from France; Lewis and Clark begin leadership of western expedition.

1804 ❖ **October 27**: Corps of Discovery reaches Hidatsa villages, builds Fort Mandan and camps for winter; eventually Sacagawea and her husband, Toussaint Charbonneau, join the expedition.

1805 ❖ **February 11**: Son Jean Baptiste is born.

April 7: Corps leaves Fort Mandan, begins journey west.

August 17: Sacagawea is reunited with her Shoshone people.

September 11-20: The Corps crosses Bitterroot Range of the Rocky Mountains.

November: The Corps reaches Pacific Coast, builds Fort Clatsop; camps here for long winter.

1806 ⬦ **March 23:** The Corps begins journey east.

June 24: In a second attempt, Sacagawea begins successful crossing back over Rockies.

July 3: Corps splits up; Sacagawea and family accompany Clark to Yellowstone River; Lewis rides north.

August 14: Sacagawea is back among the Hidatsas.

August 17: The Corps proceeds to St. Louis and disbands; Sacagawea and family remain in villages. Sometime later this year, Sacagawea probably moves to St. Louis.

1811 ⬦ **April 11:** Sacagawea and her husband leave St. Louis; most likely, six-year-old Baptiste remains with Clark.

1812 ⬦ **December 20:** A young Shoshone woman dies at Fort Manuel in present-day South Dakota. Is she Sacagawea?

❖ Shoshone Oral Tradition ❖

1806 ❖ Sacagawea leaves Charbonneau and begins to wander; eventually makes home with Comanches.

1850 ❖ From this time to about 1870, Sacagawea settles down with her Shoshone people; is reunited with Baptiste and adopted nephew, Bazil. She lives on Wind River Reservation in present-day Wyoming.

1884 ❖ **April 9**: Elderly woman known as Sacagawea dies at Wind River.

1963 ❖ Stone is erected recognizing Wind River woman as Sacagawea, a guide with the Lewis and Clark Expedition.

CHAPTER NOTES

Chapter 1

1. Harold P. Howard, *Sacajawea* (Norman: University of Oklahoma Press, 1971), p. 165.

2. Gary E. Moulton, ed., *The Journals of the Lewis & Clark Expedition*, Vol. III, August 25, 1804-April 6, 1805 (Lincoln: University of Nebraska Press, 1987), p. 228.

3 Ella E. Clark and Margot Edmonds, *Sacagawea of the Lewis and Clark Expedition* (Berkeley: University of California Press, 1979), p. 8.

4. Ibid., p. 11.

5. Howard, p. 22.

6. Moulton, Vol. III, p. 200.

7. David Holloway, *Lewis & Clark and the Crossing of North America* (New York: Saturday Review Press, 1974), p. 37.

8. Christine A. Fitz-Gerald, *Meriwether Lewis and William Clark* (Chicago: Childrens Press, 1991), pp. 15-18.

9. Ibid. pp. 19-20.

10. Ibid. p. 21.

11. Gerald S. Snyder, *In the Footsteps of Lewis and Clark* (Washington, D.C.: National Geographic Society, 1970), p. 15.

12. Howard, p. 18.

13. Moulton, Vol. III, p. 291.

14. Snyder, p. 95.

15. Gary E. Moulton, ed., *The Journals of the Lewis & Clark Expedition*, Vol. IV, April 7-July 27, 1805 (Lincoln: University of Nebraska Press, 1987), p. 299.

Chapter 2

1. Ella E. Clark and Margot Edmonds, *Sacagawea of the Lewis and Clark Expedition* (Berkeley: University of California Press, 1979), pp. 7-8.

2. Alden R. Carter, *The Shoshoni* (New York: Franklin Watts, 1989), pp. 47-50.

3. Ibid.

4. Harold P. Howard, *Sacajawea* (Norman: University of Oklahoma Press, 1971), p. 50.

5. Robert H. Lowie, "The Northern Shoshone," Anthropological Papers, Vol. II, Part 2 (New York: American Museum of Natural History, 1909), p. 183.

6. Carter, p. 35.

7. Rhoda Blumberg, *The Incredible Journey of Lewis and Clark* (New York: Lothrop, Lee & Shepard Books, 1987), p. 69.

8. Howard, p. 164.

9. Ibid.

10. Robert B. Betts, *In Search of York: The Slave Who Went to the Pacific with Lewis and Clark* (Boulder, CO.: Colorado Associated University Press, 1985), pp. 19-21.

11. Gary E. Moulton, ed., *The Journals of the Lewis & Clark Expedition*, Vol. III, August 25, 1804–April 6, 1805 (Lincoln: University of Nebraska Press, 1987), p. 228.

12. Howard, p. 16.

13. Gary E. Moulton, ed., *The Journals of the Lewis & Clark Expedition*, Vol. IV, April 7-July 27, 1805 (Lincoln: University of Nebraska Press, 1987), p. 9.

Chapter 3

1. Harold P. Howard, *Sacajawea* (Norman: University of Oklahoma Press, 1971), p. 148.

2. Gerald S. Snyder, *In the Footsteps of Lewis and Clark* (Washington, D.C.: National Geographic Society, 1970), p. 11.

3. Rhoda Blumberg, *The Incredible Journey of Lewis and Clark* (New York: Lothrop, Lee & Shepard Books, 1987), p. 31.

4. Donald Jackson, "Call Him a Good Old Dog, But Don't Call Him Scannon," *We Proceeded On*, August 1985.

5. Howard, p. 22.

6. Ibid., p. 30.

7. Ella A. Clark and Margot Edmonds, *Sacagawea of the Lewis and Clark Expedition* (Berkeley: University of California Press, 1979), p. 16.

8. Gary E. Moulton, ed., *The Journals of the Lewis & Clark Expedition,* Vol. IV, April 7-July 27, 1805 (Lincoln: University of Nebraska Press, 1987), pp. 29-30.

9. Snyder, pp. 115-116.

10. Ibid., p. 115.

11. Clark and Edmonds, p. 17.

12. Moulton, Vol. IV, p. 299.

13. Ibid., p. 309.

14. Ibid., p. 330.

15. Ibid., pp. 342-343.

Chapter 4

1. Gary E. Moulton, ed., *The Journals of the Lewis & Clark Expedition,* Vol. IV, April 7-July 27, 1805 (Lincoln: University of Nebraska Press, 1987) p. 391.

2. Ibid., p. 404.

3. Ibid., pp. 402-403.

4. Ibid., p. 403.

5. Harold P. Howard, *Sacajawea* (Norman: University of Oklahoma Press, 1971), pp. 50, 52.

6. Ibid., p. 45.

7. Moulton, Vol. IV, pp. 427-430.

8. Ibid., p. 437.

9. Howard, pp. 46-47.

10. Ella E. Clark and Margot Edmonds, *Sacagawea of the Lewis and Clark Expedition* (Berkeley: University of California Press, 1979), p. 22.

11. Ibid., p. 23.

12. Gary E. Moulton, ed., *The Journals of the Lewis and Clark Expedition*, Vol. V, July 28–November 1, 1805 (Lincoln: University of Nebraska Press, 1988), p. 100.

13. Clark and Edmonds, p. 23.

14. Ibid., pp. 27-28.

15. Ibid., p. 29.

16. Howard, pp. 61-62.

17. Moulton, Vol. V, p. 112.

18. Ibid., p. 115.

19. Ibid., pp. 183-187.

Chapter 5

1. Rhoda Blumberg, *The Incredible Journey of Lewis and Clark* (New York: Lothrop, Lee & Shepard Books, 1987), p. 93.

2. Robert B. Betts, *In Search of York: The Slave Who Went to the Pacific With Lewis and Clark* (Boulder, CO: Colorado Associated University Press, 1985), p. 36.

3. Blumberg, p. 93.

4. Ella E. Clark and Margot Edmonds, *Sacagawea of the Lewis and Clark Expedition* (Berkeley: University of California Press, 1979), p. 36.

5. Ibid., p. 37.

6. Gary E. Moulton, ed., *The Journals of the Lewis & Clark Expedition,* Vol. V, July 28-November 1, 1805 (Lincoln: University of Nebraska Press, 1988), pp. 206-207.

7. Clark and Edmonds, p. 38.

8. Moulton, Vol. V, p. 229.

9. Ibid., p. 232.

10. Gerald S. Snyder, *In the Footsteps of Lewis and Clark* (Washington, D.C.: National Geographic Society, 1970), p. 140.

11. Harold P. Howard, *Sacajawea* (Norman: University of Oklahoma Press, 1971), p. 69.

12. Clark and Edmonds, p. 41.

13. Moulton, Vol. V, p. 246.

14. Howard, p. 71.

15. Snyder, p. 140.

16. Moulton, Vol. V, p. 256.

17. Blumberg, p. 98.

18. Moulton, Vol. V, p. 268.

Chapter 6

1. Ella E. Clark and Margot Edmonds, *Sacagawea of the Lewis and Clark Expedition* (Berkeley: University of California Press, 1979), p. 45.

2. Harold P. Howard, *Sacajawea* (Norman: University of Oklahoma Press, 1971), p. 76.

3. Gary E. Moulton, ed., *The Journals of the Lewis & Clark Expedition,* Vol. V, July 28-November 1, 1805 (Lincoln: University of Nebraska Press, 1988), pp. 342-345.

4. Gary E. Moulton, ed., *The Journals of the Lewis & Clark Expedition,* Vol. VI, November 2, 1805–March 22, 1806 (Lincoln: University of Nebraska Press, 1990), p. 1.

5. Gerald S. Snyder, *In the Footsteps of Lewis and Clark* (Washington, D.C.: National Geographic Society, 1970), p. 164.

6. Howard, p. 150.

7. Moulton, Vol. VI, p. 67.

8. Christine A. Fitz-Gerald, *The World's Great Explorers: Meriwether Lewis and William Clark* (Chicago: Childrens Press, 1991), p. 82.

9. Howard, p. 84.

10. Moulton, Vol. VI, p. 2.

11. Clark and Edmonds, p. 51.

12. Moulton, Vol. VI, pp. 105-107.

13. Clark and Edmonds, p. 53.

14. Moulton, Vol. VI, p. 168.

15. Clark and Edmonds, p. 134.

16. Ibid., p. 51.

17. Moulton, Vol. VI, p. 3.

18. Ibid., p. 421.

19. Ibid., p. 426.

20. Gary E. Moulton, ed., *The Journals of the Lewis & Clark Expedition,* Vol. VII, March 23-June 9, 1806 (Lincoln: University of Nebraska Press, 1991), p. 8.

Chapter 7

1. Ella E. Clark and Margot Edmonds, *Sacagawea of the Lewis and Clark Expedition* (Berkeley: University of California Press, 1979), pp. 60-61.

2. Gary E. Moulton, ed., *The Journals of the Lewis & Clark Expedition,* Vol. VII, March 23-June 9, 1806 (Lincoln: University of Nebraska Press, 1991), pp. 105-106.

3. Christine A. Fitz-Gerald, *Meriwether Lewis and William Clark* (Chicago: Childrens Press, 1991), p. 89.

4. Moulton, Vol. VII, pp. 196-197.

5. Ibid., pp. 240-243.

6. Ibid., p. 325.

7. Ibid., p. 280.

8. Gary E. Moulton, ed., *The Journals of the Lewis & Clark Expedition,* Vol. VIII, June 10-September 26, 1806 (Lincoln: University of Nebraska Press, 1993), pp. 51-52.

9. Ibid., p. 56.

10. Ibid., p. 167.

11. Ibid., p. 180.

12. Ibid., p. 211.

13. Ibid., p. 219.

14. Ibid., pp. 225-226, 228, 237-238.

15. Clark and Edmonds, p. 76.

16. Moulton, Vol. VIII, pp. 286-287.

17. Ibid., pp. 294-295.

18. Ibid., pp. 158-159.

Chapter 8

1. Gary E. Moulton, ed., *The Journals of the Lewis & Clark Expedition,* Vol. VIII, June 10-September 26, 1806 (Lincoln: University of Nebraska Press, 1993), pp. 305-306

2. Ibid., p. 372.

3. Ibid.

4. Gerald S. Snyder, *In the Footsteps of Lewis and Clark* (Washington, D.C.: National Geographic Society, 1970), p. 200.

5. Robert B. Betts, *In Search of York: The Slave Who Went to the Pacific with Lewis and Clark* (Boulder, CO: Colorado Associated University Press, 1985), p. 119.

6. Harold P. Howard, *Sacajawea* (Norman: University of Oklahoma Press, 1971), pp. 58-59.

7. Rhoda Blumberg, *The Incredible Journey of Lewis and Clark* (New York: Lothrop, Lee & Shepard Books, 1987), pp. 124-125.

8. Howard, pp. 141-142.

9. Ibid., pp. 156-157.

10. Ibid., pp. 158-160.

11. Ibid., p. 179.

12. Ibid., p. 191.

GLOSSARY

❖ **bullboat**—A round vessel made from basket work and covered with buffalo hides.

❖ **butte**—A hill rising from the surrounding area, with sloping sides and a flat top.

❖ **cache**—A place where things are hidden or stored.

❖ **camas**—A member of the lily family with an edible bulb; known by the Nez Perces as quamash.

❖ **cradleboard**—A wooden frame worn on the back and used by many Native American women for carrying an infant.

❖ **cutlass**—A short sword with a curved, single-edged blade, once used by sailors.

❖ **fennel**—A crisp, edible root from which Native Americans made white meal.

❖ **keelboat**—A shallow riverboat for hauling goods.

❖ **militia**—A local, rather than national, army.

❖ **pirogue**—A flat-bottomed dugout; a boat similar to a canoe.

◈ **portage**—To carry boats and supplies on land.

◈ **poultice**—A moist substance (like meal or clay) usually heated and applied to an inflamed part of the body.

◈ **ravine**—a narrow valley with steep sides.

◈ **sledge**—A vehicle mounted on low runners and drawn by work animals, such as dogs or horses, and used to transport goods across ice, snow, and rough ground.

FURTHER READING

Ambrose, Stephen E. *Undaunted Courage: Meriwether Lewis, Thomas Jefferson, and the Opening of the American West.* New York: Simon & Schuster, 1996.

Betts, Robert B. *In Search of York: The Slave Who Went to the Pacific with Lewis and Clark.* Boulder, CO: Colorado Associated University Press, 1985.

Blumberg, Rhoda. *The Incredible Journey of Lewis & Clark.* New York: Lothrup, Lee & Shepard Books, 1987.

Carter, Alden. *The Shoshoni.* New York: Franklin Watts, 1989.

Clark, Ella E., and Margot Edmonds. *Sacagawea of the Lewis & Clark Expedition.* Berkeley: University of California Press, 1979.

Fitz-Gerald, Christine A. *The World's Great Explorers: Meriwether Lewis and William Clark.* Chicago: Childrens Press, 1991.

Howard, Harold P. *Sacajawea.* Norman: University of Oklahoma, 1971.

Moulton, Gary E., ed. *The Journals of the Lewis & Clark Expedition.* 8 vols. Lincoln: University of Nebraska Press, 1983-1993.

Snyder, Gerald S. *In the Footsteps of Lewis and Clark.* Washington, D.C.: National Geographic Society, 1970

⇒ INDEX ⇐